Molly Pitcher

Young Patriot

Illustrated by Gene Garriott

Molly Pitcher

Young Patriot

By Augusta Stevenson

Aladdin Paperbacks

Aladdin Paperbacks
An imprint of Simon & Schuster Children's Publishing Division
1230 Avenue of the Americas, New York, NY 10020
First Aladdin Paperbacks edition, 1986
Printed in the United States of America

10   9   8   7   6
Library of Congress Cataloging-in-Publication Data

Stevenson, Augusta.
  Molly Pitcher, young patriot.

  Reprint of the ed.: Indianapolis : Bobbs-Merrill,
c1983.
  Published 1960 under title: Molly Pitcher; girl
patriot.
  Summary: A childhood biography of the Pennsylvania
German woman who became a Revolutionary War heroine
when she carried water to American soldiers and even
fired a cannon herself during the Battle of Monmouth.
  1. Pitcher, Molly, 1754–1832—Childhood and youth
—Juvenile literature.   2. Monmouth, Battle of, 1778—
Juvenile literature.   3. Revolutionists—United States—
Biography—Juvenile literature.   [1. Pitcher, Molly,
1754–1832.   2. United States—History—Revolution,
1775–1783—Biography.   3. Monmouth, Battle of, 1778]
I. Garriott, Gene, ill.   II. Title.
E241.M7P57713   1986   973.3'34'0924 [B] [92]   86-10744
ISBN 0-02-042040-4

Illustrations

PAGE

Full Pages

"Drop it!" shouted a voice.   22

In the hand was a long knife.   52

Molly poured the water from a pitcher.   81

"The message is from my cousins."   98

"Joshua!" Molly cried.   119

The girls were busy with their samplers.   142

"I want to take care of him."   179

Molly swabbed and loaded and fired.   189

Numerous smaller illustrations

Contents

PAGE

A Lively German Girl   11

A Gay Family   26

Danger Follows
   Applause   39

An Indian Scare   56

Battles—Soldiers—
   Canteens   72

Parents and Peddlers   83

Off to a Wild Country   94

PAGE

Held by Smugglers   109

Danger at the Red Fox
   Inn   121

Molly's Home in Carlisle   132

Taxes and Masked Men   152

Molly Goes to the Fort   163

Molly's Courage in
   Battle   176

CHILDHOOD OF FAMOUS AMERICANS

Books by Augusta Stevenson

ABE LINCOLN: THE GREAT EMANCIPATOR
ANDY JACKSON: BOY SOLDIER
ANTHONY WAYNE: DARING BOY
BENJAMIN FRANKLIN : YOUNG PRINTER
BOOKER T. WASHINGTON: AMBITIOUS BOY
BUFFALO BILL: BOY OF THE PLAINS
CLARA BARTON: FOUNDER OF THE AMERICAN RED CROSS
DANIEL BOONE: YOUNG HUNTER AND TRACKER
GEORGE CARVER: BOY SCIENTIST
GEORGE WASHINGTON: BOY LEADER
FRANCIS SCOTT KEY: MARYLAND BOY
ISRAEL PUTNAM: FEARLESS BOY
KIT CARSON: BOY TRAPPER
MOLLY PITCHER: YOUNG PATRIOT
MYLES STANDISH: ADVENTUROUS BOY
NANCY HANKS: KENTUCKY GIRL
NATHAN HALE: PURITAN BOY
PAUL REVERE: BOY OF OLD BOSTON
SAM HOUSTON: BOY CHIEFTAIN
SITTING BULL: DAKOTA BOY
TECUMSEH: SHAWNEE BOY
U. S. GRANT: YOUNG HORSEMAN
VIRGINIA DARE: MYSTERY GIRL
WILBUR AND ORVILLE WRIGHT: BOYS WITH WINGS
ZEB PIKE: BOY TRAVELER

★ ★ # Molly Pitcher

Young Patriot

A Lively German Girl

THE pretty little girl's name was Mary, but everyone called her Molly. This name suited her better. She was lively, and she should have a lively name.

Everyone said she was like her parents in that way. John and Gretchen Ludwig were both jolly. So were all of Molly's German relatives. And there were plenty of them in America in 1764, the year Molly would be ten.

Most of them lived near her father's dairy farm near Trenton, New Jersey, and had come from Germany before Molly was born. They loved America and were good citizens.

They were fair people. Molly looked like her parents. She had blue eyes and yellow hair. Her cheeks were red, with a dimple in each one. The dimples were usually showing, too, for she was usually smiling.

Molly wasn't smiling this morning. She was serious. She had been counting the chickens and didn't get the right number. There should be twenty-four. She had counted only seventeen.

She counted again. It was the same as before. Then her younger brother came along and he counted. He got seventeen.

"There are seven missing. Isn't that right?"

Carl, who was just eight, wasn't very good in arithmetic. He went to school, but he had to count on his fingers to find out.

"I counted in my head," said Molly.

"You're two years older than I am. But you're not supposed to figure. You're a girl. Girls don't go to school," said Carl.

12

"I know, but I like to figure anyway. I wish I'd begun to count the chickens sooner. I've been thinking the flock seemed smaller. Some animal has been taking them, Carl."

"A fox?"

"Of course." Molly nodded.

Their father didn't agree with them. "No fox is hungry now," he said. "The woods are full of field mice, squirrels, and rabbits."

"Then a man took them," said Molly.

"That is impossible," said her mother. "Every man in this settlement is a relative. And certainly all our relatives are honest."

"It might be a dog," said Mr. Ludwig. "We'll set a trap tonight and find out."

However, they found an empty trap the next morning. And two more hens were missing. Mr. Ludwig was sure now that a dog was the thief. He said he would watch tonight.

After breakfast Mr. Ludwig went to the cattle

barn. Mrs. Ludwig started to the cheesehouse.
Carl went to school. Molly was to wash the
dishes.

She had just begun when she heard her mother
call. She went running, and so did her father.
Mrs. Ludwig stood in the door of the little one-
room cabin.

"The cheese has been stolen!" she cried. "I had
eight large pieces ready for the huckster today."

"Did you close the door last night?"

"I did, John. I thought of the chickens, and I shut it tight."

"Then it wasn't a fox," said Molly.

"Only a man could have opened the door," Gretchen Ludwig declared. "But it couldn't be any of our relatives."

John shook his head. "No, they know we have to sell cheese to make our living."

"We won't make a penny this week," said Molly.

"We'll talk about it at noon. I must finish milking now."

THE TRAVELERS AND THE CALF

When Mr. Ludwig came in at noon, he began talking at once. "I've been thinking," he said. "I believe the thief is one of these travelers passing through here."

"Do you mean the people moving to the new settlements in western Pennsylvania?" asked Gretchen.

"Yes. The Indians have made peace and there is no more danger."

"I see a traveler's wagon pass almost every day," said Molly. "I wave to the children in them, and they wave to me."

"Those men aren't thieves," said Gretchen. "They are going west to find better land. They are good people, John."

"Not all of them. Some are rascals going west to cheat the Indians, and they steal as they go along. The sheriff has had trouble with this kind. Some have even stolen cattle."

"Goodness! I hope they won't steal my calf!" cried Molly.

"They won't have a chance. I'm going after the sheriff. He'll find a traveler's wagon hidden in the woods. And it won't be far away."

"Just far enough to be handy to our chickens
and cheese," said Mrs. Ludwig.

Molly watched her father ride away. Then
she started for the pasture to look after her calf.
She had raised the calf herself, and she had
named her Blossom.

The calf was a year old now, a yearling, and
Molly thought she was beautiful. Mr. Ludwig

said Blossom should win a prize at any fair. In fact he had arranged for Molly to show the yearling at the county fair this coming Saturday.

Molly was to walk her around the ring before the cattle judges. And every Ludwig relative hoped Blossom would win the prize.

Molly had been teaching the yearling to follow her. She led her by a rope halter, but the calf didn't follow easily. She would stop to look at grasshoppers and worms. She would try to chase butterflies. She would jump away from toads and act as if she were scared.

It hadn't been easy to teach her, but she had learned to follow pretty well now. Molly wanted to give her a long lesson this afternoon. There were only two more days till the fair on Saturday.

Molly smiled as she went down the lane. She was thinking of what Blossom would do when she called. Molly loved the cute way she always ran to the gate and mooed.

This time Blossom didn't come running. She wasn't grazing, either. Molly thought she had gone to sleep in the shade. It was a very warm day, and Blossom often could be found under a shade tree on warm days.

There was no calf under the trees on the woods side. There was an opening in the rail fence, however. It was quite large enough for a calf to go through.

"I must tell Father about this," Molly thought. "The rails must have rotted and fallen. Of course Blossom had to see what was in the woods. Maybe she smelled water and went to the creek."

The cows had made a path there from the pasture, and Molly followed it. She saw signs as she went along. Leaves had been crushed and twigs had been broken.

She was sure she was on the calf's trail. She would know in a few minutes, as soon as she reached the creek.

Now she was almost there. She could see the water through the trees. Then she saw something that frightened her—a traveler's wagon! But she saw only the white top. And it was almost hidden by trees.

Could this be the thief's wagon? Her father said it would be near. Molly went to the edge of the bank to see better, but she kept out of sight behind the bushes. Quietly she parted the branches to look.

She saw the wagon more plainly. It was on the other side of the creek. Then she looked down at the shore. And there was Blossom! But she wasn't having fun with butterflies.

A rope was around her neck, and a big rough boy was leading her. He had her at the water's edge and was trying to make her cross. But the calf pulled back.

Molly knew the reason. Blossom had never

20

crossed a creek before, and she was afraid. The water wasn't deep, but it was somewhat noisy. It was swirling around big rocks and stones.

The boy waded in, but the calf refused to follow. Then he came back and kicked her with his heavy boot. Molly couldn't stand this. She came from the bushes in a hurry.

"Stop that!" she called angrily. "You'll hurt her!"

"I'll do what I please! She's my calf!"

"You took her from our pasture!"

"I didn't! I found her loose in the woods."

Molly was on the shore now. She had scrambled down the bank in a minute. She tried to get hold of the rope, but the boy pulled it away.

"I'm going after my father!" she cried.

"Go on! He won't get this calf. My pa won't let him take her."

"I'll tell the sheriff. He's my uncle, and he's seen my calf," said Molly.

"He won't see her again."

"Why won't he?"

"I won't tell you," the boy said stubbornly.

"I know! You're going to leave. You'll take her along."

"Sure I'll take her."

"The sheriff will follow you. He'll get you, too. And he'll bring you back and put you in jail," Molly threatened.

"Go home! If you don't, I'll throw this at you!" The boy picked up a large stone.

"Drop it!" shouted a voice from across the creek. A man had come to the other bank. He was a mean-looking man with a scowl on his face. "I told you to drop it!" he repeated.

The boy dropped the stone, but he was ugly about it. "She's claiming the calf, Pa!" he said.

"I heard her. Hand it over."

"What do you mean?" cried the boy. "You said——"

"Never mind what I said. I don't want the sheriff coming here," the man shouted.

"But I found the calf! She was loose in the woods!" the boy protested.

"Did she lift the rails from the fence?" Molly asked sharply.

The boy scowled at Molly. "You think you're smart, don't you?"

"That's enough talk," ordered the boy's father. "Give the girl the rope or I'll come across the creek. You know what you'll get if I do."

The boy threw the rope down, but he turned to Molly angrily. "I'll get even with you," he yelled. "You'll see! I'll get even!"

Molly was a little frightened. She knew that the boy was very upset. When he turned away, she picked up the rope and led Blossom quickly toward home. She didn't stop until she had the calf safely in the barn.

Then Molly ran to tell her mother what had

happened. She couldn't tell her father yet, because he hadn't returned.

"We'll have to keep the calf in the barn," said Mrs. Ludwig. "We can't let her run in the pasture as long as those people are about. You must not go to the pasture either, Molly. That boy is angry with you and intends to get even. We don't know what he might do the next time he sees you."

A Gay Family

John Ludwig was surprised when he got home from the sheriff's. He had expected the cows to be in the barnyard. Molly always brought them from the pasture early.

The cows were just coming down the lane. And his wife was driving them! What was this? She should be getting supper.

A little later she was telling the reason, and he was listening gravely. "It is bad, very bad," he said when she had finished. "You were right to keep Molly in the house. She must stay out of the pasture."

"When is the sheriff coming?"

"I didn't see Brother Kurt. He was taking a prisoner to the jail in Trenton. He won't return till Saturday. I'll see him at the fair."

"There's no telling what this strange boy will do. He threatened to get even with Molly. He must be fifteen or so from what she said."

"We'll have to guard her and the calf, too."

Now Carl came from the stable. "There won't be any chickens stolen tonight, Father. Molly and I moved them. We put them in coops in the stable."

"You were smart to think of that, Carl."

"I didn't think of it," Carl admitted. "Molly made me help her move them."

Mrs. Ludwig and Carl helped with the milking and chores. At last the work was finished, and they started to the house.

"Look!" Carl exclaimed. "There's my teacher on the road!"

"Ask him in to supper," said Mrs. Ludwig.

"He is new—we haven't invited him yet to eat with us."

"Isn't this a poor time, with Molly cooking?" said Carl.

"Well, he is here and it is suppertime," said Mrs. Ludwig. "It will be all right."

"You are right, he must be invited," said Mr. Ludwig.

Mrs. Ludwig went in the back door. Mr. Ludwig and Carl went to the front gate.

"Master Remy!" John called. "Please come in. I am happy to see you here."

"I was out for a walk," said the young schoolmaster. "You have a fine view from this hill. I came up just to see it."

"So you like this country?" Mr. Ludwig asked.

"Very much, and I like the people, too."

"I was afraid you wouldn't like our German ways. You are English," said Mr. Ludwig.

"But we are all Americans, sir."

"That is indeed true. How do you like to teach German children?" Mr. Ludwig asked.

"I've never had a better school. I've never had such obedient pupils," answered Mr. Remy.

"All German children are obedient. German parents are strict."

Then Mr. Ludwig invited the teacher to supper, and Mr. Remy accepted. He wondered if the Ludwigs would be as gay as their house.

It was yellow brick with a roof of red tiles. The shutters and wide front door were blue. Two blue benches stood on the porch. And everything was so clean it was shining.

However, it wasn't the kind of house Germans built in their settlements. They usually had two stories. This house had one.

Mr. Ludwig saw Mr. Remy's puzzled look and smiled. "You expected to see a German house, didn't you?"

"I knew you were German——"

"I am, but my wife is Dutch. She wanted a Dutch house. And I must say I like it myself. I like to wear the Dutch wooden shoes, too, for work. They last longer than leather, and they are easier to clean."

The supper bell rang just then. Mr. Remy waited on the porch while the others took off their shoes.

"They are noisy on our bare floors," Mr. Ludwig explained.

"We just wear stockings in the house," Carl added. "We leave our shoes here."

"Shall I take mine off?" asked Mr. Remy.

"No, no," Mr. Ludwig replied. "Leather shoes are not noisy." He led Mr. Remy into the hall and motioned to a bench. "We'll sit here for a moment." Then he explained why Molly was getting supper.

"I'll guard the barn tonight," Mr. Remy offered. "I have a musket, and I can shoot."

Carl liked that. "I'm going to tell the boys at school."

"I don't shoot my pupils, Carl."

Then Mr. Remy knew that Mr. Ludwig and Carl were lively from the way they laughed.

Now Mrs. Ludwig and Molly came to greet the schoolmaster. Both wore clean linen work dresses and were in their stocking feet.

"The supper is on the table," said Mrs. Ludwig. "Will you please come?"

They went into the main room of the house. It was a large room where the Ludwigs cooked, ate, and sat. Mr. Remy was delighted—it was so clean and bright.

The floor, tables, and benches were almost white from scrubbing. The two windows were paper, but the paper was clean. The fireplace hearth was clean. Even kettles and skillets were a shiny black.

The family and the schoolmaster sat at a long narrow table on benches without backs. They helped themselves from the platter of hot corn meal mush. They had horn spoons and wooden bowls.

"This isn't a company supper," said Gretchen Ludwig.

"We have mush and milk nearly every evening at home," Mr. Remy replied. "My mother says it is good food."

"It is—if it is cooked right," Mrs. Ludwig agreed.

"I always have good luck with my mush," Molly bragged. "It's as smooth as butter every time."

"I'm sorry to say it," said her father, "but I fear there is a lump in mine."

"A lump!" exclaimed Molly. Her face grew red. "A lump!" she repeated.

"It looks like one to me. It has never happened

before in this family, Master Remy. I hope you haven't found one in yours."

"No, sir, mine is smooth," he answered.

"I *never* had lumps in my mush before," said Molly. "I stirred it a long time today."

"He's teasing you, Molly," said her mother. "Your mush is as light as a feather."

John smiled and patted his daughter's hand. "Your mush is so good I must have more."

Everyone took a second helping. Then Molly said she had a surprise for them—hot hoecakes and spiced crab apples.

"We eat them together," Mrs. Ludwig explained.

Mr. Remy tried it. "It is delicious!" he exclaimed. "I will tell my mother about this. She will want to know how you made the hoecakes, Molly. Did you stir the corn meal much?"

"Yes, sir. And it has to be stirred with a hoe," Molly said.

34

"Molly!" cried her mother.

Then the lively Ludwigs laughed. And young Ralph Remy laughed with them.

When he left a little later, Molly and Carl went with him to the gate.

"Well, I hope you can teach your calf to follow you, Molly," he said. "Is she quick to learn?"

"No, sir, she's slow," answered Molly.

"Then she must be like some of the pupils in my school."

Carl hung his head.

"Oh! I didn't mean you, Carl," said Mr. Remy. "But you could learn faster if you would study your reading at home."

"I can help him, Master Remy," said Molly. "I know how to read a little. My two older brothers taught me."

"Why aren't they in my school?" asked the schoolmaster.

"They aren't here. They're grown up. Joseph

is a soldier and Joshua is a sailor. They didn't like to milk cows," said Molly.

"I see. Well, I hope your yearling wins the prize, Molly. I'll be there to see you parade."

"I've got a new dress to wear. It's a Dutch dress. It's the kind Mother wore in Holland when she was a little girl," Molly announced.

"My mother will want to see your dress. Maybe that will persuade her to go with me."

"Tell her I'll ride the calf around the ring. Then she'll be sure to come."

Mr. Remy laughed and went away. "That girl is as gay as her house," he said to himself.

The Ludwigs began to get ready the next morning, Thursday, for the fair. Gretchen made pies, cookies, and cakes, and Molly helped her. Then she helped her father clean the large two-wheeled cart. The family would ride in this.

In the afternoon Molly gave Blossom lessons. But they had to stay in the yard. Mr. Ludwig said even the lane was dangerous. A stone could be thrown from the trees.

In the evening the whole family polished the horses' bells. These were small, but there were ten for each of the two horses. This kept the Ludwigs busy till bedtime. Molly heard the bells ringing in her ears until she went to sleep.

Friday morning she helped her mother with their 'Fair Dinner.' It was afternoon before she could give Blossom her last lesson.

"Blossom followed you very well," said her father.

"She didn't jump at a thing," said Carl.

"I hope she does as well tomorrow," said her mother.

Now it was time to get Blossom ready for the parade. Molly picked the burs from the calf's tail and combed it. She washed her. She brushed her again and again.

The yearling was clean from head to hoof.

Clean fresh straw was put in her stall. Then Molly tied her in it.

"She can't get loose," said Carl. "You know how to tie a rope."

"Ropes can be cut," said Molly.

"Don't be afraid of that," said her father. "I'll fasten the barn door so no one can get in. And if I hear a noise in the night, I'll go out with my musket. Blossom will be safe."

Danger Follows Applause

THE LUDWIGS were up at dawn Saturday, but they didn't dress for the fair. They put on their work clothes for the feeding, milking, and chores. Molly went to the barn with her father.

"I didn't hear a noise in the night," he said. "And the door looks just as I left it."

It was dark inside. They couldn't see anything distinctly. Molly dreaded to go in for fear her calf wouldn't be there. So she stood in the door and called softly.

"Blossom! Blossom!"

"Moo-moo!" answered the calf.

Then Cousin Jacob came. He had offered to

guard the stock today, and he had brought his musket along. "I'll watch your pasture like a hawk," he said. "But why aren't you taking one of your fine cows? There are Lily and Pansy and Ivy. Any one of them would get a prize!"

"Yes, I think they would. But the judges wouldn't give two prizes to the same family. And I want Molly to get one. She's worked hard to raise her calf."

Cousin Jacob helped put Blossom in a small cart. He helped hitch this to the back of the large cart. He carried the picnic dinner from the house. And Molly packed it in a wooden chest under the driver's seat.

Then, of course, he helped the Ludwigs eat breakfast. He said he didn't go to fairs any more. In fact he hadn't gone since the time his calf's tail was cut off.

"My goodness!" cried Molly. "Why would anyone do that?"

"To keep her from winning the prize, my dear. That's been done several times at fairs."

"Don't worry, Molly," said her father. "There will be a cattlekeeper today. He'll watch your calf so that nothing will happen to her."

41

A little later Mr. and Mrs. Ludwig, Carl, and Molly were dressed in their best clothes and climbing into the cart.

"You look like a rainbow in the sky," Cousin Jacob told Molly. "And I hope you have as gay a trip as the gay clothes you are wearing."

"This isn't the dress I'll wear in the ring," said Molly. "That's in the cart, wrapped up in a sheet. And my new wooden shoes are beside it."

At last they were ready to start. Mr. Ludwig cracked his long whip. The two horses started together. The wheels began to roll. The bells began to tinkle.

The Ludwigs didn't leave their farm often. So all four sat on the driver's seat. This was their chance to see things along the way. And if any one of them missed a bird, it was because they were talking.

It was almost noon when they reached the fairground. The cattlekeeper took charge of Blos-

42

som. She would be put in a pen and fed and watered.

Then all the Ludwig relatives joined John and his family. They were gaily dressed also. Mr. Remy said they looked like a great bouquet when he stopped to say hello to them.

The families put their dinners together at the fair. So now their tablecloths were spread on the ground, and the food was brought from their carts. Molly and her cousin were as busy as bees.

"There's enough food here to feed an army," said Mr. Remy, smiling.

"When we're through there won't be enough for an ant," said one of Molly's jolly uncles.

They all wanted Mr. Remy to eat with them, but he had to refuse. He said he was with his cousins, Dr. and Mrs. Irvine, from Carlisle, Pennsylvania.

"Bring them with you," said the generous Ludwig women.

"Yes, bring them along," said the generous Ludwig men.

He had to explain. "We ate before we came, at my mother's in Princeton."

"I saw the doctor's wagon and six horses," said Kurt Ludwig, the sheriff. "With a team like that, he didn't need to start early."

"Like the poor Ludwigs, with only two," said John, smiling.

"So poor they are starving," joked Mr. Remy. "I can't see the tablecloths for the food on them."

Everyone laughed, and then Mr. Remy explained about Dr. Irvine's handsome team. "He had to bring a big covered wagon from Pennsylvania. They will take a load of heavy furniture back to Carlisle. Mrs. Irvine's parents gave it to them."

"They will need six horses," said Sheriff Ludwig. "The roads are bad all the way to the mountains. The trip will be a hard one."

44

MOLLY PARADES WITH HER CALF

At two o'clock Molly went into the ring with her calf. The bridle was only a blue silk ribbon, but Blossom followed nicely. The crowd liked this and applauded.

"It's a fine calf," said one farmer. "I'd give it the prize."

"Molly's mother ought to have a prize also," said his wife. "She made Molly's dress."

The blue cotton skirt was full. The blue waist was trimmed with white lace. Her little apron and cute little cap were white lace. A pretty chain of blue beads was around her neck.

Her two long golden braids were tied with blue ribbon. And, of course, she wore wooden shoes. She carried a small bouquet of flowers in her left hand. In her right was Blossom's blue ribbon bridle.

"Isn't her dress pretty!" exclaimed a girl cousin. "I want one just like it."

"So do I," said another cousin.

"I'd want one myself if I were a girl," said a boy cousin.

Cousins weren't the only ones who liked Molly's dress. There was a strange lady there who loved it. She was Mrs. Irvine, Mr. Remy's cousin. She and her husband were now visiting his home.

"Isn't that dress cute?" she exclaimed. "The little girl is cute in it, too. I love the way she smiles. Look at her dimples, William! She's as pretty as a picture."

"She is," Dr. Irvine agreed. "She is polite, too. Look how nicely she bows to the cattle judges."

"Tell us about her, Ralph," said the lady. "I'm really interested in the girl. I'd like to do something for her. Are her parents able to give her much?"

"I'm afraid not, Anne. Her father owns a small dairy farm. He can't make much money."

"Just a mere living," said Dr. Irvine. "Are there other children?"

"Yes, a boy younger than Molly. And two older boys. She'll be ten next month."

"Does she go to school?" asked Anne.

"No, her parents don't believe in sending girls to school."

"Very few people believe in that," declared the doctor.

"There's a school for girls in Carlisle," said Mrs. Irvine.

"There's no use talking about that, Anne. Her parents wouldn't let her leave home."

"They might let her come for a visit. We could bring her back next summer."

"I doubt if the girl would come. German children are devoted to their parents."

"It wouldn't do any harm to talk to her, William. Could you manage it, Ralph?"

"I can bring her over here when she comes from the ring. I'd better start to the gate now. It will be hard to get through this crowd."

Things just didn't happen that way. Molly's father was waiting to take her to the cattle judges. They wanted to know more about the yearling. By the time Mr. Remy reached the gate she was gone.

He happened to meet Mrs. Ludwig, however. He told her what his cousin wanted to do. "She has taken a fancy to Molly," he added.

"Please tell the lady I thank her, and I am proud she liked my daughter. But we couldn't part with Molly for a long visit."

So the Irvines didn't meet Molly at this time. And Anne Irvine went back to her home in Carlisle disappointed.

THE HAND HELD A KNIFE!

Molly had answered the judges' questions and had started back to the cart. She told her father she wanted to put on a different dress. But she changed her mind and went instead to see Blossom.

She found the pen easily—she knew the row faced the woods. There was no one about. The keeper was busy taking other yearlings from pens and leading them to the ring.

Blossom was lonesome. Molly could tell by the way she acted and mooed. So Molly patted her and talked to her as long as she could.

"We can't leave till the judges give the prizes," she said. "But it's nice and shady here. You can look out into the woods, Blossom. You can see birds and squirrels. I believe I see a rabbit right now. I see its white fluffy tail in the brush."

Then her face grew pale and her knees grew weak. A boy stepped out of the woods—a big boy in a white shirt. He was the thief who had taken her calf!

She closed the door to the stall quickly. It was only a half door with space above and below. But at least it would hide her for a moment.

Molly stayed as quiet as she could. She remembered only too well the last time she had seen this boy.

She watched him through a crack in the side wall. Perhaps he had come to see the cattle. But he passed their pens without a glance. He was coming straight to Blossom's!

She had time to get away. She could go out the back way, behind the pens. But she wouldn't leave her calf here alone. She'd keep this boy out of the stall if she could. He was older, but she was strong. Father said she was as strong as an ox.

Molly looked about for a club. There wasn't even a loose board. She took off one of her wooden shoes. Then she crouched under the low feed trough and waited.

She couldn't watch the boy now. There were no cracks between these boards. But she heard the thud of his bare feet. She could tell that he was getting closer. The next instant his hand

came over the half door. And in the hand was a long knife!

At the same time a bare foot was thrust under the door into the stall. Then a wooden shoe hit that bare foot hard. The boy groaned and dropped his knife.

Molly jumped up. "Help! Help!" she shouted.

The keeper came running. But the boy had disappeared. Molly told the man what had happened.

"I saw that strange boy hanging around," he said. "He asked me how to find your calf's pen."

"I thought he was going to kill her."

"He wouldn't have dared. Every farmer in the county would have hunted him."

"Was he going to cut off her tail?" Molly asked.

"Maybe, to get even with you," he said.

"I'm going to tell Uncle Kurt right away," said Molly. "I'll give him this knife. It will be proof."

The sheriff said it was good proof, along with

a bruised foot. "I'll get that boy before sunset," he declared. "I'll send the whole family out of New Jersey. They won't spend another night here. I'm going after them right now."

He hadn't been gone ten minutes when the cattle judges gave out the prizes. Molly's calf was first in the yearling class, and Molly received the prize.

This was three bundles of barrel staves. Molly was delighted. The staves were the same as money. They could be exchanged for almost anything.

Half the way home she thought about the things she would get for her mother and father and Carl. Then she heard the others singing, and she sang with them.

After a while Molly was too sleepy to sing. She had had an exciting day. Now she was tired. She just listened to the music of the bells.

Tinkle, tinkle, tinkle, tinkle.

Tinkle, tinkle, tinkle——
Tinkle—tinkle——

The day had been exciting for everyone in the Ludwig family. Mother and Carl were tired, too. Soon everyone except Father, who had to stay awake to guide the horses, was asleep. Father alone listened to the tinkle of the bells the rest of the way home. He had to wake up the others when the little cart finally pulled up at the farm at dark.

An Indian Scare

Just at dinnertime one noon a visitor came to the dairy farm. He was Amos Ludwig, John's brother. Everyone was glad to see him. But why didn't he bring his wife and two little girls?

"I couldn't, this time," he said. "I had to ride horseback on account of the bad road. And I came on very special business."

As they sat down at the table, Gretchen made excuses for the food. "We have only pork, sauerkraut, and dumplings, Amos."

"That suits me exactly. I'm glad you didn't know I would be here."

The food was on a large wooden platter.

They ate from wooden plates. But they had china cups for their sassafras tea.

"It's nice to drink from these cups," said the visitor. "They seem to make the tea taste better."

"Mother brought them from Holland," said Molly. "We just use them when we have company."

"They are too fine to use every day. I'm proud you got them out for me."

"We haven't seen you for a year or so," said John. "And you live only fifteen miles away!"

"It might as well be fifty. The road is too bad for a cart. That's why I can't bring my family. But it's no farther from there to here than from here to there."

The others laughed. Then John said he couldn't leave his dairy even for one day. And Amos said he was glad he had become a gardener. It didn't tie a man down like cows. "I've had time to build a fort," he added.

"Fort!" exclaimed the others.

"We call it that because it's so strong. It's made of logs, but it's no small cabin. I built it large enough to hold my neighbors."

The others didn't understand. So he explained. "We live on the bank of the Delaware River. Across is Pennsylvania. The Indians have been attacking settlers there. So I decided to be ready for them."

"But those settlers lived out near the mountains," said John.

"Suppose the warriors come on east? Suppose they cross the Delaware?"

"They'll never get that far. The King's army is out there. It is holding the Indians back."

"Well, yes, it is just now. I believe your son Joseph is in that army."

"He is, and I am sure he is doing his share of the fighting."

"Where is your son Joshua now? Is he still

sailing a freight boat from Trenton to New York?"

"He was the captain of one," replied Gretchen. "But we haven't heard from him for a long time."

"So long we are worried," John added. "As soon as I can find time I'm going to see the dockmaster at Trenton. He might be able to give me information."

"I go to Trenton every week to sell my vegetables. I could see him for you and send you word."

"I'd be glad to have you do that, Amos."

"And now," said Amos, "I must tell you about this very special business of mine. I am supposed to take Molly home with me for a visit—if she would like to go. And I will bring her back."

"Oh, I wish I could, Uncle Amos! I want to see your fort. And I want to play with Frieda. We're the same age, you know."

"I do know. You'll both be ten years old to-morrow. Your Aunt Christy has baked a big cake for you and Frieda."

"Please let me go, Mother! Please, Father! I've never visited anyone."

"I can let her have my riding horse for two weeks," said John.

"But we have no sidesaddle," said Gretchen. "And it's a long trip."

"I'd rather ride bareback, Mother. I've been riding that way all my life."

"Well then, I consent."

"I can pack my clothes in Father's saddlebags," said Molly. "I'll get them right away."

THE FORT AND THE SECRET CLOSETS

By mid-afternoon Molly and Uncle Amos were on their way. It was very tiresome, jogging along over the rough roads, but Molly kept think-

ing about her cousin Frieda and the birthday cake Aunt Christy had baked for the two girls. She kept wondering about the house, too.

"Will it really look like a fort?" she said to herself. "I can hardly wait to see!"

By early evening the two riders had reached the big log house on the riverbank. It had two stories, and there was a spring of cold water in the cellar.

"We won't have to go outside for water if Indians come," said her cousin Frieda. "Father built the house over the spring on purpose."

"Molly, you must be hungry and tired after your long trip," Aunt Christy said gently. "After you've eaten, you and Frieda must get to bed. Then tomorrow morning we'll show you the house and everything you want to see."

Molly had a warm supper of mush and milk. Then she was tucked into bed. It wasn't long before she had drifted off to sleep.

"Happy birthday!" Aunt Christy said to both Molly and Frieda as they sat down to eat breakfast the next morning. "I hope your day is a happy one!"

"Thank you, Aunt Christy," replied Molly. "I'm sure mine will be."

Aunt Christy showed Molly the two large secret closets upstairs. "We can hide here if Indians get in the house," she explained. "You see, each closet has a little opening for air."

The farm girl was delighted with the wide Delaware River. She loved to stand on the bank and watch it flowing by. She loved to look across at Pennsylvania.

"Just think, I'm looking at it!" she would say to Frieda. "I'm going to tell everyone back home that I saw Pennsylvania every day."

Molly couldn't understand why there were so many sailboats. Some were small, some were large. Some had one sail, some had two.

"Where are they all going, Aunt Christy?"

"That's the best way for people to travel, Molly. The roads are so bad they go by water. Freight is shipped by water, too. Some of those boats are cargo sloops."

"One might be Joshua's. I wish he could land here."

"This shore is too rocky. All boats land at the Trenton docks. Your uncle is going there to-morrow. He'll find out about your brother."

It was late the next evening when Amos returned. The girls had gone to bed.

"I didn't have to go to the docks today, Christy. I met the dockmaster on the street. He said he had never heard of a captain named Joshua Ludwig."

"Perhaps Joshua is just a sailor."

"He had never heard of any sailor by that name. And he said he knew them all."

"Then Joshua's boat must have been lost in a storm. He must have gone down with it."

"That was what I said. But the master declared no captain or sailor by that name had been lost at sea within the last five years."

"I can't understand it, Amos. What do you think happened?"

"I think Joshua's in trouble of some kind. I think he's afraid to land at the docks."

"It might be. We mustn't let Molly know."

"No. Nor John nor Gretchen. I'll tell Molly I didn't get down to the docks. And that is the truth. I didn't."

64

"Tell her some of your Indian stories tomorrow night. That will get her mind off Joshua."

"I'll tell them every night then."

So from this time on Amos Ludwig told Indian stories in the evening. They weren't all scary, but Christy wouldn't allow four-year-old Emma to hear them. She put her to bed early. Then the others sat about the fire and listened.

This evening he talked about Indian scouts. "They go ahead of the warriors," he explained. "They hide in or near a settlement. Then they count the white men living there. And they count the white women, too."

"Would they count Frieda and me?" asked Molly.

"Yes indeed! They might seize you girls and take you back to their camp to work."

"You'll frighten the children, Amos."

"That's just what I want to do. Girls, if you ever see an Indian prowling about, you must not take any chances by staying around. You must run for home."

"I saw some Indians at the fair once," said Molly.

"They were friendly Indians," said her uncle. "But there are none of them in New Jersey now. They all went over the mountains."

"He means they joined the tribes over there— the ones who were fighting white men," said Aunt Christy.

"Goodness! I'll be afraid to go outside," said Molly.

"You needn't be afraid," replied Uncle Amos. "There's no real danger now. But there will be if the Indians ever decide to cross over the mountains and come this way. No one knows what to expect from Indians. We can only hope that they will not come."

"That's enough, Amos. The girls will dream about Indians. Now then, it's time for bed."

66

The two weeks were up. Molly was to go home today. Her uncle was to take her, but he couldn't be ready for an hour yet. So she would have a few minutes to get some more shells from the river shore.

This time the two girls took Emma. They didn't want to, for they were in a hurry. But she cried, so there she was walking along with them.

They reached a path they could take down the steep bank. Frieda started down and Emma followed. Molly was last. She saw Emma take hold of a bush. Then she saw something move behind it—something large and brown.

Molly knew what this meant. An Indian was hiding there! An Indian scout! She was frightened, but she didn't lose her head. She tried to think of a way to get the girls back home.

She thought fast as she went down the path. Suddenly she stopped and called out, "A snake!

A snake! Come back, girls! I won't go down there! Come back!"

She climbed up the bank fast. Frieda followed her, but Emma didn't move.

"Where snake?" little Emma asked.

Then Molly did something that Frieda couldn't do because she wasn't strong enough. She went back down the path. She lifted the child and swung her over one shoulder.

Emma laughed, and thought this was fun. Molly wanted to run, but Emma was too heavy.

"What kind of snake was it, Molly?" Frieda asked.

"I don't know."

"Was it a long snake?"

"Hush, Frieda. I don't even want to think about it."

Just as Molly was putting Emma down in the kitchen, her uncle came in from the yard. His face was serious and his voice was sharp.

"I've just heard bad news," he said. "A neighbor came to tell me. He heard it in Philadelphia yesterday. The Indians have come over the mountains again. They are coming this way."

"They are here!" cried Molly. "There's one hiding in the bushes on the bank. I saw him!"

"Molly! Are you sure?"

"Yes, Uncle Amos." Then she told her story. And because she was excited, it sounded as if she had actually seen an Indian.

When she finished, her uncle took a large

cowhorn from the mantel. Then he stood in the open door and blew it three times.

"That's the signal for the neighbors," Aunt Christy explained. "It's to warn them of an Indian attack. They'll come here at once."

"You can't go home now, Molly," her uncle said. "It wouldn't be safe to travel. We might be surrounded by Indians. I think they crossed the river last night and are hiding in the forest."

"They might spread out all over the country," said Aunt Christy. "They might attack several places at the same time."

"Will anyone warn my parents?" asked Molly.

"I hope so," her uncle replied. "They can go to the fort near Trenton."

"I know, but they won't go there unless they are told of the danger."

"I am sure they will hear, Molly."

The girl knew he wasn't sure. He didn't want to talk about it. He left the room quickly.

"You might as well unpack your bundles," her aunt advised. "There's no telling when you can go."

Molly didn't unpack. She was going home to warn her parents. She didn't dare to tell her relatives. They wouldn't let her go. She'd watch for a chance to get away.

Then the neighbors began to arrive. In a short time the big house was filled with them. Men and women were talking. Children were playing. Babies were crying. Dogs were barking.

There was so much confusion it was easy for Molly to slip out. Soon her bundles were in the saddlebags, and she was riding away.

She knew she wouldn't be missed for some time. And then it would be too late to pursue her. She should be home by suppertime, if the Indians didn't get her.

Battles—Soldiers —Canteens

Mr. Remy was having supper at the dairy farm that evening. He knew they were expecting Molly and her uncle. Mrs. Ludwig was keeping food warm for them. And a bed had been made ready for Amos.

Then suddenly the kitchen door opened, and they saw a pale and frightened girl.

"Mother! Father!" Molly cried. "The Indians are coming! Uncle Amos said they would attack every settler in New Jersey."

Her mother hurried to her and drew her in. "There's no danger now," she said. "The Indians are not coming. It was just a rumor."

She took Molly's hand and led her to a seat by the fire. "Your hands are cold—you are trembling."

"I was afraid I wouldn't get here in time. I thought you wouldn't know."

"We were warned," said her father. "A rider came by with the message. He had been sent to all farms in this settlement."

"We were going to the fort near Trenton," said Carl. "We had our bundles ready. Then we didn't go."

"Master Remy had come with another message," Gretchen explained. "He told us the danger was over and we need not leave our homes. The Indian bands had been defeated in a battle with the King's troops. And the warriors had fled over the mountains."

"The general sent a soldier to tell us," added Mr. Remy. "He came from the battlefield, with the news, Molly."

"I wonder why Amos doesn't come in," said John. "He's had time to put up the horses."

"He didn't come, Father. I slipped away— none of them knew."

"And you rode all that way alone!" cried her mother. "You poor child! I expect you thought there were Indians all about you."

"There was one on the riverbank before I started. He was hiding behind bushes."

"That's strange!" exclaimed Mr. Remy. "The Pennsylvania shore was guarded for miles. Not even one canoe could have crossed near your uncle's farm."

"Uncle Amos thought he was a scout who had crossed in the night," said Molly.

"He would have been seen and shot. It was a bright moonlight night."

"But I saw him myself! I was the one who told Uncle Amos."

"You saw him!"

74

"Yes, Master Remy. I saw something large and brown move behind a bush."

"Did you see his face?" asked Mr. Ludwig.

"No-o. I just saw his brown arm or leg. He moved when Emma grabbed the bush."

Mr. Ludwig smiled. "I'm afraid little Emma spoiled a nice nap for a groundhog."

"Groundhog!" exclaimed Molly.

"Yes, my dear. They are as brown as Indians. And they are fat fellows this time of year. The one you saw more than likely was full of your uncle's corn."

"Ha, ha!" laughed Carl.

Molly's face grew red. She seemed ready to cry. Her voice trembled when she spoke. "The neighbors will blame me—so will Aunt Christy and——"

Her father interrupted. "If anyone is to blame, it is my brother. He should have questioned you. He blew his horn too soon."

"But someone ought to tell them, Father. The neighbors will want to go home."

"They all know by this time," said Ralph Remy. "The governor's riders were to go all over the countryside to tell the good news."

"And we'll never be frightened again," declared Gretchen. "At least not by Indian warriors. Please tell her about it, Master Remy."

"The governor will send a new army to help the troops out there. The Indians won't dare to fight so many. So he expects them to sign a peace treaty."

"Then Joseph can come home," said Mrs. Ludwig.

"And I can visit Frieda again," said Molly.

MOLLY GETS A NEW NAME

It took a long time to get the new army ready. Wagons had to be made. Horses had to be bought. It was hard to get enough muskets and powder. And soldiers had to have clothing, bedding, and food.

It was the spring of 1765 before the army was ready to start west. Molly Ludwig was ten and one half before soldiers began to pass the farm with their supply wagons.

There was a long hill to climb before they reached the Ludwig farm. It was a hard pull for the horses. There were six for each wagon, but the loads were heavy.

So the drivers always rested them at the hilltop. And the soldiers rested here, too. This was just in front of the Ludwig house with its yard full of blooming tulips.

"Look!" said an officer. "The house is clean, the dooryard is clean, and so is the barnyard. This would be a good place to get water."

Mr. Ludwig let them help themselves to the bubbling water in the springhouse. They drank from a large gourd dipper. They then went on their way.

The next group of soldiers found water waiting for them at the roadside. Molly had carried a bucketful out. Carl had carried the dipper. The soldiers were very grateful and thanked them both.

After this the children met every group of soldiers with the water bucket and dipper. Mr. Ludwig brought water for the horses. So soldiers and drivers were grateful.

Once a young soldier started to tease Molly. "Hi, Wooden Shoes, come here!" he called. "I want to see how you walk."

The captain heard him and went to him at once. "I'll have no more of that kind of talk," he said sharply. "If I do, I'll leave you in the nearest jail."

Sometimes the soldiers asked questions. They were all young. Some were only fifteen. They never had been away from home before, and they wanted to know things.

"Little girl," said one of the soldiers, "is it true the Dutch can foretell the weather?"

"Yes, sir. My mother is Dutch and she can."

"Can you tell when the rain is due?"

"Yes, sir. It will rain when fish jump from the water. When birds fly close to the ground. When snails come out. And when the cat washes her face in the morning."

No one laughed. No one even smiled. They all believed in signs themselves.

Another soldier asked, "Is it true the Dutch know how to cure sick people?"

"My mother knows—she's Dutch."

"What would she do for measles?"

"Cut an onion open and leave it in the room."

"I've got warts on my trigger finger," said another. "Do you know how to get rid of them?"

"Rub the warts with half a raw potato. Then

throw that same half of potato over your left shoulder."

"I'm going to try it. Thanks, little girl."

Other soldiers had questions, too, but they didn't have time to ask them.

"Forward march!" shouted the sergeant.

So there was a good deal of grumbling as they went along.

"I wanted to ask her what to do for my corns," said one soldier.

"I wanted to ask about my boil."

"I wanted to ask about mine."

Finally the captain spoke. "Maybe I'd better go back and get the girl. I don't see how you fellows can fight Indians. Not with your boils and warts and corns."

Usually Molly didn't have time to talk. She was too busy filling canteens. She poured the water from a pewter pitcher. And every soldier was grateful.

"Thanks, Molly! Thanks, Molly!" Not one of the boys failed to thank her.

Sometimes she would miss some of them. Then these soldiers would call, "Molly! Pitcher! Pitcher!"

One day a captain noticed a bashful young soldier with an empty canteen. "Molly Pitcher!" he shouted, "Molly Pitcher! Fill this one, please."

The soldiers thought this was funny. "Good-by, Molly Pitcher!" they called as they left. "Good-by, Molly Pitcher!"

Molly thought it was funny, too. She smiled and waved as long as she could see them.

Parents and Peddlers

MR. REMY didn't open his school in September this year, 1765. The boys were too excited about the army supply wagons and soldiers. And there was still too much talk about Indians.

By October things were quiet. There were no more soldiers passing through. So Mr. Remy opened his school on the third. He was waiting for his pupils now in the log schoolhouse.

The morning was so chilly he had made a fire in the Dutch stove. Mrs. Gretchen Ludwig had loaned it to the school, and he was proud of it. But he had to smile when he looked at it. In fact he couldn't see it all at one glance.

He could see the part that was in the room. The other part was outside. The stove had been set into the back wall. The firebox came out into the room.

The stove door was outside, and he had to go into the yard to fire it. However, this was better than the smoky, sooty fireplaces in English schools, he thought.

"You can trust the Dutch to find a clean way of heating," he said to himself.

He began to wonder why the pupils didn't come. They had always been on time last year. In fact they had come too early. By seven o'clock the room would have been filled.

Now it was eight, and not one boy had come. Now it was eight-thirty, and the room was still empty. What had happened? At nine he decided to lock the door and go home.

Then came six parents, all fathers of his pupils. They greeted the schoolmaster gravely.

Then they sat down on the wooden benches. Mr. Remy could see that they were worried.

John Ludwig spoke first. "Master Remy, we have come on sad business. We can't send our boys to your school this year. We can't afford to pay you."

"I might take a little less."

"Even that would not help us. We can't pay you anything. We are sorry. You have been a good teacher."

The others nodded and John went on: "The governor has put a new tax upon us. And, now that times are hard, we don't know where we'll get the money."

"I didn't know about this tax," said Mr. Remy.

"We didn't know until yesterday. That is the reason we couldn't get word to you. We have been taxed for the expense of the Indian War."

"We are willing to pay our share," said Otto Ludwig. "It is good to have soldiers to defend us. But the governor has demanded too much from us. It will take all my crops to pay my share."

"It will take all of mine," declared Jacob Buler.

"And mine! And mine!" cried others.

"It will take more milk than my cows can give," said John. "We can't make enough butter and cheese to pay this tax."

"I know how it is with all of you," said Mr. Remy. "And I am truly sorry. I wish I could teach for nothing."

"No," replied John, "we would not allow that. You have your living to make. If times grow better we will want you to return."

"Yes, we will!" said Otto.

"We will!" said the others heartily.

The fathers had much respect for Mr. Remy. Someday, they hoped, they could send their children back to his school.

That very day Mrs. Ludwig explained to Molly about the hard times. "You're almost eleven," she said. "It's time you understood."

"I do, Mother. I know why the boys can't go to school this year."

"Then you will understand why I must make more butter and cheese to sell to the huckster. You can take my place in the kitchen and get the meals. Do you think you can do it?"

"Of course I can! I know how—I've helped you ever since I can remember."

However, it wasn't so easy as Molly had thought. Getting a meal all alone wasn't like helping her mother. There was so much to remember. The chicken must not be fried too long. The goose must not be baked too hard. The sausage must not have too much pepper. The smearcase must not have too much salt. Oh, there were a thousand things she had to learn.

The cleaning was easier. In a short time Molly was as particular as her mother. Mrs. Ludwig declared she was worse about the kitchen floor.

Carl agreed to this. "She fusses at me if I forget to take off my shoes. She won't have even one speck of mud on the floor."

"I'm just like Molly about my cattle barn," said his father. "I won't have anyone tracking dirt in there. So try to remember your shoes, son. You'll be helping to keep the house clean."

Carl remembered pretty well all winter. But spring brought other troubles. Every week there were peddlers. And each one tried to get into the kitchen to show his wares. And they didn't take off their muddy shoes.

The weather was warm, and the kitchen door had to be open. So Molly had to watch like a hawk to keep them out.

One day a peddler almost made it. Molly was on her knees scrubbing the floor. Her back was to the open door. There was a soft knock, but she didn't hear it. She was scrubbing too hard.

"Good morning," said a strange voice.

It was an English voice—it sounded like Master Remy. Molly jumped to her feet and turned. There on the step stood a strange peddler. He was holding up a chain of beads and smiling.

"I'd like to show you this chain, Miss. The beads are blue like your eyes."

Then he put one muddy shoe inside.

"Don't! Don't!" Molly cried.

"Don't what, Miss?" asked the peddler.

"Don't come inside!" said Molly.

"I just want to show you this chain."

"Don't walk across to me!"

"Well, then, why don't you walk across to me? You really should see it."

"I can't, sir. Don't you understand?"

The peddler looked puzzled. Then, suddenly, he thought he understood. "Oh!" he said. "I'm sorry. I didn't know you were a cripple."

"I'm not," said Molly. "I've just scrubbed the floor. I'm afraid I'd track it."

Now the peddler looked puzzled again. "I thought floors were made to walk on," he said.

"You're English," said Molly. "That's why you think that. I'm part Dutch."

"I'd hate to be even part Dutch if I couldn't use my peg on a floor." He held up his other leg to show his wooden peg. "What would you do, Miss, if you had one of these?"

When Molly saw the peg leg, she felt very sorry for the peddler. "I'm sorry, sir," she cried. "Please come in. I'll help you."

She crossed the room quickly. Her bare feet made tracks on the floor, but she didn't care now. She held the door wide open so the peddler could hobble in.

"Sit here on this bench by the table. Now please show me your chain. Oh! It is pretty! I had a blue bead chain once, but I lost it."

"I thought you'd like it."

"I do, but I can't buy it. We can't buy anything pretty. Father has to use all his money for his taxes."

"I've been hearing that from everyone. Why, I haven't made enough to buy my dinner today. Times must be very hard."

"I could give you some smearcase and souse," Molly offered. "But if you're English perhaps you don't even know what they are. Smearcase is a kind of soft, runny cheese, and souse is pickled pigs' feet."

"I'm not really an Englishman," the peddler explained. "I just talk like one. I was a sailor on an English ship. That's how I lost my leg. A mast fell on me in a bad storm."

"I'm sorry to hear that, sir," said Molly. "I hope that won't happen to my brother. He's a sailor, too."

Molly set some dishes on the table. "Here are the smearcase and souse," she said. "I hope that you will like them."

"I love them," exclaimed the peddler. "I was brought up on them in Holland."

Molly was surprised. "Oh! You are Dutch!"

"Yes, indeed," said the peddler.

Then Molly gave him blueberry bread with butter for dessert. The peddler was delighted. "The berries are so close they touch!" he cried. "I won't leave a crumb of it."

"I picked the berries myself," said Molly. "So they didn't cost anything."

"This chain will cost you nothing, either. Take it, please—it is yours. You have been kind to an old sailor with a wooden peg. I'm happy to give it to you."

"I'll be proud to wear it, sir."

When Mr. Ludwig heard the story he smiled. Then he thought of his own sailor son. "I wonder why Amos hasn't told us what the dockmaster said about Joshua."

"I expect he forgot to go," said Gretchen.

Off to a Wild Country

MOLLY needed a new dress. She hadn't had one for a long time, and she had been growing fast. Every dress she owned was far too short and much too tight.

She was almost twelve, and she was large for her age. She was even taller than her mother. So Mrs. Ludwig's old dresses couldn't be made over for her.

Of course Mr. Ludwig's clothes were made over for Carl. And Gretchen had patched John's clothes and her own. But she couldn't make short skirts longer. And she couldn't weave cloth for new clothes without yarn.

The Ludwigs had sheep and they raised flax. For years Gretchen had woven the goods for their clothes. But this year the wool and flax had to be sold to pay taxes.

Mrs. Ludwig had saved short lengths of yarn. She had been knitting stockings with these all winter. She had a plan.

"I'll have a dozen pairs ready for the huckster," she told her husband one evening. "I'll trade them for dress goods for Molly. She must have a new dress, John. Or else she'll have to stop growing."

"It's a shame all our wool and flax have to be sold. And my own family needing clothes!"

"You can blame the governor for that. He put this extra tax on us."

"No, he had nothing to do with it. It is King George who is to blame. He is the one who makes tax laws. The governor has to obey him."

"Well, he is the King of England. And England owns America. So I suppose he thinks he owns Americans and can make us do what he pleases."

"He'll find out differently some day."

"What do you mean?"

"I mean we'll rise up against him. All the farmers here are ready now. They think Americans should decide about their own taxes."

"I hope and pray it will happen."

Mr. Lukes, the huckster, came the next week. But he wouldn't buy the stockings. Neither would he trade his dress goods for them.

"I've got a cart full of woolen stockings," he said. "Every woman in the country has been knitting them. Besides, I've sold my business. There'll be a new huckster next week. Maybe he'll take them."

It was a great disappointment to Mrs. Ludwig and Molly. As soon as Mr. Lukes had gone they both cried. And John Ludwig felt very sad.

"Molly," he said, "you shall have a dress if I have to sell a cow to pay for the cloth."

"No! No! You can't afford to sell one of your cows, Father."

"We'll wait till next huckster day," said Gretchen. "The new man might take them."

It wasn't long until the new huckster came. Molly and Carl were watching for him and saw him when he drove up in his wagon.

"My goodness!" cried Molly.

"Look, Mother!" cried Carl.

"Oh!" cried Gretchen. "Oh!"

It was no wonder they were surprised. The huckster was Mr. Ralph Remy!

"I couldn't get a school," he explained. "So I bought out Mr. Lukes." He then examined the woolen stockings. "I'll take them all," he said. "I have some customers who want them."

"May I trade them for dress goods?" asked Mrs. Ludwig.

"Yes, indeed! I have several different colors. Shall I bring the bolts out?"

"No, Molly can look at them. Choose any color you like, dear."

Molly climbed into the wagon. Carl had already gone off somewhere. Then Mr. Remy spoke softly. "Mrs. Ludwig, I have a message for you. I don't want Molly to hear. Can we walk on a little way?"

They walked a few steps and stopped. Then Mr. Remy went on. "The message is from the people who want the stockings. They are my cousins from Carlisle, Pennsylvania, Dr. and Mrs. Irvine."

"I remember. They wanted to take Molly home with them."

"They have just come east again. And they still want her. They asked me to tell you. They said they would treat her like a daughter. They will give her everything she needs."

"We can give her nothing."

"I know how it is with you, and with all farmers in New Jersey. But these hard times haven't struck Carlisle yet. So my cousins still have plenty."

"I wish she had gone with them then. She has had to work too hard. And there is nothing else for her if she stays with us. She may have to plow the fields."

"She would have no hard work at the Irvines'. She would just help Anne with the cooking and cleaning, but that wouldn't be much work. They eat plain food and their house is small."

"Molly wouldn't be happy if she wasn't helping and doing her share."

"She'll have fun, too. Anne is already planning a party for her, so she will meet girls her own age."

"Well, I wish she could go. Your cousins are good people. But Molly helps us to make our living. She does all the cooking and housework. I have to make cheese and——"

Mr. Remy interrupted. "The doctor will pay her wages. He will pay for the whole year now. It is enough for your taxes."

"Mr. Remy! Enough for our taxes?"

"More than enough."

"I will talk with John tonight and with Molly also. I am grateful to you, Master Remy."

"I am a 'Master' no longer. I am Ralph the huckster to you, lady."

Both smiled. Then they went back to see about the goods for Molly's dress.

THE STORM BROKE

One morning a month later a big covered wagon rolled down a street in Trenton. Each horse had bells on its harness.

Three sailors heard the tinkle, tinkle, and

101

stopped to look. "It's a beautiful wagon," said one. "See how it's painted red and blue!"

"It's pretty enough for a boat," said another. "That white top could be a sail."

"Aye," agreed the third sailor. "And it could do as many tricky things as a sail. What will the people in the wagon do if the top fills up with wind?"

"If that happens, they'll need a sailor," said the first young man.

"Aye! Aye!" said the others.

The wagon now stopped in front of a small shop. "I can buy our food for the journey here," said the driver. "Shall I hitch the horses?"

"No, I can hold them," said the woman.

"I'll clean the feedbox," said the pretty blond girl. "And I'll pack the food away. I always did that for Mother when we went to the fair."

Dr. Irvine gave the reins to his wife. Then he climbed down from the high seat.

"Be sure to get enough bacon and eggs," Mrs. Irvine said. "We'll have to cook along the way, Molly. The inns are far apart."

The doctor nodded and went into the store. Molly Ludwig had already climbed over the seat and down into the wagon. She had found a dust-cloth and had begun to clean the large feedbox.

It was ready when Dr. Irvine came with the food. Molly put it in the box carefully. The doctor was pleased.

"You know how," he said. "Some girls would have put the bacon on top of the butter."

Molly laughed. "I knew better than that when I was a baby."

"I believe it," said Mrs. Irvine with a smile. "You certainly know the right way to do things."

By this time they were all on the driver's seat. Then the doctor drove down to the dock on the Delaware River. Molly thought of Joshua, but there was no time to ask about him.

The ferry barge was waiting. It had been fastened to a small boat with a stubby sail. This boat was to tow the barge across the river.

The bargemaster was in a hurry to start. And so was Dr. Irvine. There were black clouds in the sky. Both men feared a storm. Six horses wouldn't be easy to manage if they became frightened. Neither would the wagon if the barge began to pitch and roll.

"I'm not sure we can make it," the bargemaster said. "The Delaware is very wide here."

Dr. Irvine looked at the sky again. "The clouds are breaking up now. I think we can get across."

"Just as you say, sir. But let us be quick with the loading."

At last the wagon and horses were aboard, and the barge began to move. The bargemaster was on the sailboat. Dr. Irvine stood in front of his two lead horses and held their bridles. Mrs.

Irvine sat on the driver's seat holding the lines. Molly sat by her.

"Look at the clouds, Molly!" she exclaimed presently. "They are blacker than ever. I'm afraid it will rain."

"Shall I close the cover?"

"Yes, please. I don't want our furniture to get wet."

Molly closed the wagon cover, both front and back. "The rain can't get in now!" she said when she climbed back to the driver's seat.

"It's too bad we couldn't take this furniture with the other, two years ago. But there wasn't room in the wagon. I really wanted to come in our coach this time. It would have been a much easier trip."

Molly scarcely heard her. She was watching the black sky. "I don't think it will rain," she said suddenly. "The clouds look like wind clouds to me."

Almost the next moment the wind was shrieking about them. It was lashing the water and making great waves. A gale was blowing! The stubby sail of the little boat carried them faster and faster toward the shore.

Just then something terrible happened. The wagon cover filled with wind and billowed out like a large balloon.

The small sail wasn't much good now. It was the balloon that was pulling the boat! And it was pulling it straight toward some large rocks! The barge would be dashed against them if its course couldn't be changed.

"Cut the ropes!" the bargemaster cried. "Let the wind out the top! We'll all be killed!" He was shouting at the top of his voice.

The doctor didn't dare to leave the horses. The roar of the wind and water had frightened them. Mrs. Irvine didn't dare to drop the lines. And Molly knew she couldn't untie the hard knots in time. The rocks were too near. She would have to cut the top. It would be dangerous. She might be blown into the river.

Molly didn't let fear stop her. She ran past the plunging horses. She got a knife from the doctor. Then back to the wagon and up to the wagon cover she went. One long slash did it. The wind was let out. The cover fell.

Now the bargemaster could control the barge. He was able to turn it away from the rocks.

"And it's thanks to you, little girl," he said later. "You saved us."

Dr. and Mrs. Irvine were amazed at Molly's bravery and quick action.

Dr. Irvine spoke first. "If you hadn't been with us, Molly, we might have been killed."

Then Mrs. Irvine added, "We are very happy that you weren't hurt, my dear, and we are grateful to you for saving our lives."

Held by Smugglers

THE GALE was over in a few minutes. The doctor expected the bargemaster to land. But he sailed on down the river instead.

"Land here!" shouted Dr. Irvine.

"No! No! Bad country!"

Dr. Irvine couldn't understand what the man meant. There was a fairly good shore here. He saw only a few large rocks. But the bargemaster sailed on.

Again the doctor shouted, "Land here! Land here! I order you to land here!"

Then the bargemaster obeyed, but he showed he didn't like it. He brought the barge to shore and tied it. Then the doctor went ashore and joined him.

"I didn't want to put you off here, Doctor. This is smugglers' country. No sailor or boatman ever lands here. He might never get back."

"Nonsense. Smugglers don't harm travelers. All they want is to sneak their goods in without paying a tax to the King's office on the docks."

"Suppose they thought you were an officer. Suppose they thought you had been sent to spy on them. You'd soon see whether they would harm you or not."

"If I should meet any, I would explain how I happened to land here."

"They might not believe you."

"Do you see that big creek just above? Do you see another one north of that?"

The doctor nodded.

"Now look south. How many streams do you see in that direction?"

"Three, clearly, and two, faintly."

"All empty into the Delaware. And they are all large enough for cargo boats. A ship can slip in any one of these streams and be out of sight in five minutes. Smugglers can unload behind the trees and vines without any King's officer to see them."

"Well, the officers must know the smugglers are here. Why don't they arrest them?"

"For a very good reason. The officers don't want to be shot."

"Well, I can prove I'm neither an officer nor a spy."

"You are determined to land here?"

"I must. I have sick patients waiting for me in Carlisle."

"Very well, sir. But I have warned you."

A little later the boat was sailing away with the barge, and the passengers were on the shore. Ahead was a high bank covered with trees.

There was no road to be seen. But there was a path to the bank, and the doctor decided to follow it. He was sure there would be a road on the top.

"I'll be back in ten minutes," he said.

Mrs. Irvine and Molly went to work on the torn wagon cover. It took them some time to sew up the slit. Then they had to put the cover in place and tie it to the wagon sides. Still Dr. Irvine had not returned.

"It wouldn't take him *this* long to find a road," said Mrs. Irvine. "I'm afraid something has happened to him."

"I'll look for him if you don't mind," Molly offered.

"Well, you might go as far as the bank, but don't go up. We don't know what is on the top."

Molly started but came back at once. "He's coming," she said softly. "But there are two men behind him, and each one has a musket."

112

The doctor came to the wagon. The two men followed. Their faces were grim.

"We can't leave now, Anne," he said. "These men refuse to let us go." His face was grave.

"The captain has to see you first," said one sharply. "And he's busy now. Search the wagon for firearms, Job."

No one spoke during the search. When it was over Job had the doctor's musket.

"Bring it along," said the first man. Then he turned to Dr. Irvine. "Remember what I told you. Stay away from that bank."

They left now and soon disappeared in the woods. Then the doctor explained, but he kept his voice low. "They are smugglers. I think their ship had just landed. I saw men carrying bales and bags up the bank. They probably have a warehouse up there."

"Did you explain why we had to land here, William? Did you tell them everything?"

"Of course. They laughed when I told them about our wagon-top balloon. They said it couldn't happen."

"I'd like to show them the slit we sewed up," said Molly.

"They wouldn't believe you cut it. They said a wind that strong would blow a girl into the river."

"Maybe it would blow a thin girl. But I'm heavy. I weigh a lot."

"Thank goodness you do!" exclaimed Mrs. Irvine.

"Yes, thank goodness!" said the doctor.

Now Job came back, but he did not have the doctor's musket. He said the captain was holding it. "And he'll be likely to keep it if he's not satisfied with your story. He said he would listen to you now. Come along."

"Don't worry, Anne," said Dr. Irvine. "I'll make the captain understand."

Mrs. Irvine and Molly watched the men go along the path until they disappeared.

"Do you suppose the captain wears earrings?" asked Molly. "And a sash and a sword?"

"I don't know. I've never seen the captain of a smugglers' ship."

"Goodness," exclaimed Molly, "I hope he won't be fierce."

"I hope he won't be angry."

"Could he keep us here?"

"I don't know what he'll do with us. It's too bad we had to land here."

"Just think of meeting smugglers, Mrs. Irvine! I never expected to see one as long as I lived."

"I don't want to talk about it, Molly. I'm too worried."

The doctor returned sooner than Mrs. Irvine and Molly expected. And he carried his musket. "Everything's all right," he said, "and we're free to go. The captain knows now that I'm no spy. And I know he's not what he seems to be."

"Can't you tell us as we drive along, William?"

"We can't leave just now. He told us to wait till a man came to show us the way to the road."

"Did he wear earrings?" asked Molly.

"He's not a pirate, Molly. He's not even a real smuggler. He's a patriot. He's trying to force the King to take off the tax on sugar."

"Does the captain know that hardly anyone can afford to buy sugar on account of the tax?" asked Mrs. Irvine.

"He certainly does, Anne. That's why he's smuggling it into the country from the West Indies. And he doesn't stop at any dock to pay the tax to the King's officers."

"Hooray!" cried Molly.

"So he can sell the sugar for a low price. Neither he nor his men are making any money on this. And they are determined to keep the King from making any."

"Do you think they will?" asked Mrs. Irvine.

"They are doing it now. There's a barn on the bank half full of this cheap sugar. He's giving a bag to you, Anne. Here's Job with it now."

"You will have to hide it, sir," said Job. "You

could be arrested if this kind of sugar was found in your wagon."

Job put the bag of sugar in the wagon. Molly went to work to hide it. She put a feather-bed over it. Over this she piled quilts and clothing.

"I'll sit on top of that if anyone tries to look," she declared.

While she was still busy, the captain came.

"I wanted to meet Mrs. Irvine," he said.

Molly turned quickly. "Joshua!" she cried. "Joshua!"

In a flash she was out of the wagon and in her brother's arms.

HOW IT ENDED

Dr. Irvine and his wife told Joshua why Molly was with them. Then Molly told him about the Ludwig family.

"I'm a patriot, too," she added.

"Good! I'm glad to hear that, little sister."

"So are Mother and Father. I'm going to tell them about you and what you are doing and your men and everything."

"No, no! They must not know. It might get them in trouble. They might be asked questions. Promise me you won't tell them."

"I promise, Joshua."

It was time to go and good-bys were said. The doctor cracked his whip, and the horses started. But they only walked, for Job was leading them to a road.

There were tears in the young captain's eyes when the wagon disappeared. He loved his little sister. He hated to see her go. And he knew, too, that he might never see her again. He was indeed in a dangerous business.

Danger at the Red Fox Inn

It was noon when the Irvines and Molly left the smugglers' camp. The road was fairly good. The doctor didn't want to waste any time, so they ate a cold lunch as they traveled. And they talked about Molly's brother.

"He looked like you, Molly—the same blue eyes and yellow hair," said Mrs. Irvine.

"He used to be jolly like me. But he wasn't this morning. He hardly smiled."

"He isn't in a jolly business," said the doctor. "Patriots haven't much to smile about now."

"The Tories do all the smiling," said Mrs. Irvine. "The King favors them in every way."

"Of course, Anne. They want England to continue to rule America. They think the English King will keep their purses filled."

"I don't know any German Tories," said Molly. "All my relatives are patriots."

Before long the road became so rough they couldn't talk. All afternoon they were jolted and bounced about. They were glad when they came to an inn at dusk.

The doctor looked at the sign over the inn door. "This is the Red Fox Inn," he said. "The landlord's name is George Grimes."

"It's a dirty-looking place," said Mrs. Irvine. "I hate to stop here, William."

"There's no other inn within a day's journey. But we won't be alone. I see three freight wagons in the yard. That means there are teamsters to keep us company."

He had barely stopped the horses when the landlord hurried out. Mr. Grimes bowed and smiled and bowed again. He tried very hard to be pleasant, but the doctor didn't like him.

"I can let you have two rooms, sir," said the landlord. "They are very nice rooms. I'm sure you will be pleased with them."

"We'll want only one," the doctor decided. "I shall sleep in the wagon."

"But that is not necessary, sir! The inn is not crowded."

"It is necessary for me. I must save money whenever I can. I am a doctor."

"You like to joke, Doctor. Anyone who travels like this does not need to save. Six horses! Why, a prince would like to drive such a team!"

"Four horses could not pull this wagon."

"It is larger than most travelers own. And now about your room, sir. There are wagoners here who will want it."

"You may let them have it, Mr. Grimes. Is supper ready?"

"Oh yes, sir! And what about your horses?"

"I'll tie them to these posts and feed them myself. That will save money."

The landlord didn't like this, but he smiled and led Mrs. Irvine and Molly into the house.

Six wagoners were eating at the long rough table. Mrs. Irvine and Molly were told to take an empty bench.

They tried to eat the food, but it was terrible. The meat was as tough as leather. The dumplings were as heavy as lead. The cabbage was burned. The bread was sour. The apple pie was the worst they had ever tasted.

Molly took two apple cores and some peelings from her piece. She couldn't cut the crust, not even with her meat knife.

"You couldn't dent this crust with an ax," she said. "You could drive a wagon over it."

The teamsters laughed so loudly the landlord hurried in to see what was going on.

124

Molly was scared now. She hoped they wouldn't tell him. She had good luck this time. The men just smiled and went on eating.

Dr. Irvine came in as the wagoners were leaving. He had a chance to whisper to his wife while the men were paying for their supper.

"You needn't go back to watch, Anne. Joshua and Job have come. They will guard our wagon. Don't tell Molly. She might say something."

Then he said aloud, "I brought two extra quilts for you. I think it will be cold tonight."

MOLLY HEARD THE THIEVES TALKING

Mrs. Irvine and Molly followed the landlady up the steep stairs to their bedroom. It was so dark they could hardly see the bed. And the woman didn't want to leave the candle.

"You both can undress in the dark," she said. "Candles cost money."

"I'll pay you extra for it," said Mrs. Irvine. "Leave it or we won't stay."

"Oh, I'll leave it then, but be sure to blow it out when you go to bed. If you want anything in the night, call me. My room is next to this. Just knock on the wall."

Mrs. Irvine closed the door and began to examine the room. She and Molly spoke softly. They were sure Mrs. Grimes was listening.

"We can't lock the door, Molly, but we can be locked in. The bolt is on the outside."

Mrs. Irvine walked over to the bed with the candle in her hand. "Look at those dirty sheets," she said. "We won't sleep in them. We won't even undress. We'll just take off our shoes."

Molly didn't know what to think about the way Mrs. Irvine was acting. "Are you afraid of something?" she whispered.

"I don't like the looks of things here, Molly. Something is wrong."

126

Mrs. Irvine spread one of her own quilts on the bed. She and Molly lay down on it and used the other quilt for a cover. They didn't blow out the candle, either.

Molly was so tired that she went to sleep at once. Suddenly she woke up.

Mrs. Irvine was shaking her. Molly opened her eyes. Then Mrs. Irvine put her hand over Molly's mouth and whispered in her ear. "Listen! They're planning to rob us!"

Molly heard voices on the other side of the thin wall. It was the landlord and his wife. They spoke softly, but Molly heard every word.

"There's money in that wagon," said the man. "I'm sure of it. The doctor wouldn't take a room. He pretended he couldn't afford it. He just wanted to stay out there on guard."

"Then we can't go through his belongings."

"Yes we can. I'll slip up on him and give him a blow. When he comes to, he'll think some of the teamsters hit him and robbed him."

"We must wait till the wagoners are asleep."

"That will be around midnight. I'll stay downstairs to watch."

"Then I'll get some sleep. Wake me when it's time."

"Shall I lock the woman and girl in?"

"Not till they go to sleep. I'll draw the bolt."

Now a door closed softly. There were soft footsteps in the hall. Then the stairs squeaked, and Molly and Mrs. Irvine knew that Mr. Grimes was going down.

"Wait till the landlady is asleep," whispered

Mrs. Irvine. "Then we'll try to get out. We must warn the doctor. We'll carry our shoes."

At last they heard the landlady snoring. "Now!" whispered Mrs. Irvine. They opened their door a crack and listened. There wasn't a sound.

"Look at the candle," Molly whispered. "It's nearly out. We ought to go now—it's late."

"Wait! I'll see if Mrs. Grimes is awake."

As Mrs. Irvine went to the wall, Molly slipped out the door. When the woman came back Molly was gone. Mrs. Irvine was frightened. Had the landlord locked her up?

Then suddenly Molly was back. "I went down to see what he was doing," she whispered. "He's asleep by the fire."

Mrs. Irvine and Molly crept down the creaking steps slowly. They reached the main room. The landlord still sat by the fire, and he was still asleep. They were afraid he would awake when they passed him. But there was no other way to get out of the building.

Slowly and silently they passed Mr. Grimes, and he slept on. As they went toward the door, every old board squeaked. They expected, with every step, that Mr. Grimes would awake, but fortunately he slept on. He sat quietly as they passed in front of him.

At last they were across! Now they had lifted the latch! Now they were outside! They didn't stop to close the door. They ran for the wagon yard in their stocking feet.

It was moonlight—they found their wagon easily. Just as they reached it a man came from behind it. And it wasn't Dr. Irvine!

"Joshua!" cried Molly softly.

"S-sh! Speak no names," the captain whispered. "The doctor needed sleep."

In another minute Dr. Irvine was wide awake. The next minute he was hitching up the horses. Joshua and Job were helping.

There were quick good-bys softly said. Then the Irvines and Molly were on their way to open country and safety in the moonlight.

Molly's Home in Carlisle

For days the travelers had been jolted and bounced. Several hills had been so steep the horses could hardly pull the wagon up them. The riders had to climb on foot.

Every time this happened Mrs. Irvine said the same thing. "I wish I had wooden shoes like yours, Molly. These rocks hurt my feet. I'll never wear leather shoes on another trip."

Once Dr. Irvine accidentally got off the road and drove into a marsh. The horses couldn't pull the wagon out. Someone had to go back to the road for help. It was then that Molly's wooden shoes really came in handy.

It didn't matter if they got wet. They wouldn't shrink so that she couldn't get them on again. She waded through the marsh to the road.

The first wagon to come along was a freight wagon, with four horses and one teamster. He'd be glad to help, he said. He had been helped out of mudholes himself—more than once, too.

He unhitched his four horses and took them to the edge of the marsh. Then the ten horses pulled the wagon out and back to the road.

The doctor was grateful and offered to pay. But the teamster refused to take any money.

"No, we're all in it together, sir. The King lets us all sink in the mud and mire. He doesn't lift a hand to help us."

"You sound like a patriot," said Dr. Irvine. "I'm glad to know you—I'm a patriot myself."

"Every teamster is. We all blame King George for these terrible roads. He gets our tax money. Why doesn't he spend some of it on roads?"

"He may be forced to some day."

"I want to help when that happens. I want to be right there."

Then came more days of bouncing, jolting and climbing. Hills became mountains. Inns were so far apart that the travelers had to sleep in the wagon. And they cooked many meals by the roadside.

In spite of hills, mountains, rivers, and creeks they finally reached Carlisle. They were on a low hill now, looking down into the town.

"Why, it's on level ground!" exclaimed Molly. "I thought someone told me Carlisle was on a mountain."

"It's in a valley," replied Dr. Irvine. "It is surrounded by mountains, but they are miles away."

"I didn't know there would be so many houses. And what is that with the four towers?"

"That is Fort Lowther. It's the largest fort

in these parts. It has stood against many Indian attacks. We'll pass it on our way."

They began to descend to the valley. Suddenly Molly remembered. "I've heard of this fort, Doctor. My brother Joseph sent us a message about it. A returning soldier brought it. He told us that Joseph was here for a week. It was when he came west to fight Indians."

"All soldiers stopped here, Molly. It was a resting place. They had had a long hard journey. They had another to the battleground around Fort Pitt."

"They also rested here when they went back," said Mrs. Irvine. "There are fifty bunks in the fort."

"Here we are!" Dr. Irvine called a little later. "Look at the gate, Molly. Do you see how wide it is? Does that tell you a story?"

"I don't understand——"

"Why, the story of people leaving their homes

in a hurry. The story of Indians pursuing them with tomahawks."

"Oh! I see! Two wagons could go through at one time!"

"There's another gate on the other side as wide as this one," said Mrs. Irvine.

"Four wagons at one time!" cried Molly.

"And many other wagons just behind," added the doctor. "And every man whipping his horses to beat the Indians to the fort."

"I didn't know it was like that out here. Aren't you afraid we'll all be scalped?"

"There's no danger now," replied Mrs. Irvine. "Carlisle was on the very edge of the frontier then. There was nothing but Indian country beyond. It is different now. There are other towns west of us."

"There is no longer any danger from Indians," declared the doctor. "The trouble was settled two years ago. Their chiefs signed a peace treaty with the white men. So we will keep our scalps, Molly."

"Many of the soldiers went home," Mrs. Irvine added. "The fort would be full of them at times."

"My brother didn't come home."

"Perhaps he is still in the garrison at Fort Pitt," Dr. Irvine said. "It had to be guarded, or the Indians would have torn it down." He reined up the horses now, and the wagon stopped.

"Here we are!" cried Anne Irvine. "This is our home, Molly."

Molly was astonished. She looked at the house, but all she could say was "Oh! Oh!"

THE EVERYDAY-DRESS PARTY

Molly had expected to see a log cabin. She had been told there was nothing else in the west. So when she saw a stone cottage, she was surprised. She didn't know there was a stone quarry in Carlisle, and that stone was as easy to get as logs.

She was surprised to find such a nice house out in the wilderness. There were four rooms on the ground floor. One was the doctor's office. The others were sitting room, dining room, and kitchen.

On the second story there were two bedrooms. And every room in the house had glass windows. Molly had been used to paper windows.

She was delighted with the two windows in her room. "Why, I can see right through them!" she cried. "I can see trees and streets and houses!"

The first thing was to find a good place to hide the sugar. Mrs. Irvine finally decided to put it in the cubbyhole under the stairs. She didn't think any Tory would find it there.

"Do you have Tories out here?" asked Molly quickly.

"If there are any they keep it secret," the doctor replied. "We are all patriots, so far as I know. There is one man here I suspect, though. He is Richard Fleming. I tell you this, Molly, because you will probably meet his daughter Cynthia. She is your age."

"They haven't lived here very long," added Mrs. Irvine. "They came from Philadelphia. Mrs. Fleming said they were looking for good farm land to buy."

"There's plenty of farm land for sale in this valley," said Dr. Irvine, "but Mr. Fleming hasn't bought any. There is something odd about the Flemings. He doesn't do any work, but the family lives like rich people. Be careful what you tell Cynthia, Molly."

"What could I tell her?" asked Molly.

"Oh, you might forget and say something about your brother Joshua," said the doctor.

"And get him into trouble? I wouldn't do that, Doctor! No one could make me tell on him. I'd just like to see anyone try!"

"So would I," said Mrs. Irvine smiling. "I think he'd run for cover."

In a day or so everyone in Carlisle had heard about Molly Ludwig. They knew why she had come, and most of them understood.

Hard times had struck the valley while the Irvines were away. It was like New Jersey now. People didn't know how they could raise the

140

money to pay the last tax the King had demanded for the Indian War.

Mothers were making over clothes for their families. Few girls had anything but everyday dresses. They were lucky if they still had good ones they could wear.

So when Mrs. Irvine invited them to meet Molly, she called it an "Everyday-Dress Party." When the day came, Molly, in her work dress, met six young girls in their everyday dresses.

The Carlisle girls had wondered if Molly would wear wooden shoes. But she was wearing leather shoes like theirs. The peddler's blue beads were around her neck. Everyone said she looked pretty.

Mrs. Irvine thought the girls all looked pretty. Their dresses had just been washed, starched, and ironed. And so well washed, so well starched, and so well ironed! They were as pretty as fine dresses, Mrs. Irvine thought.

The girls seemed to like Molly from the very first. She was kind and nice to them. Besides she was jolly and laughed at everything.

Seven girls had been invited, but Cynthia Fleming didn't come. None of the girls knew why. And they wasted no time talking about her. They were too busy with their samplers.

They had brought these to the party along with the yarn to work them. Of course, Molly had hers. She had started it in New Jersey. The girls wanted to see it, and she wanted to see theirs. So they passed them around.

The samplers were made of canvas. This was strong but loosely woven. Each had the alphabet at the top. The letters were to be embroidered with colored yarn. There were also decorations on each one. And these were to be embroidered with different colors.

Lydia was making vines on her sampler.

Mary was making flowers.

Susan was making flying birds.

Rachel was finishing a strange-looking house.

Betsy was embroidering a strange beast.

Sarah's sampler had a sea horse. The fish's head looked like that of a tiny horse.

Molly had started this verse:

> When I was Young and in My Prime,
> You see How Well I Spent My Time.

Each girl told the colors she was using. Some wanted advice. Did the others think red and blue would look right in one word? Others asked about yellow and green. And so on and so on.

All the while, needles and yarn were forming letters. And letters were forming words. The girls hadn't wasted a minute up to the time refreshments were served.

Mrs. Irvine led them to the dining room. They sat on benches at the table. There was a mug of sweet milk for each one. They could help themselves to the warm cookies on the platter.

Molly had made them herself. She had used the sugar which was hidden under the stairs. But this, of course, was a secret. The girls were supposed to think the cakes were made with honey.

They were all delighted. They said they hadn't had sweet cakes for two years. Not since the King had put the tax on sugar.

"We can't afford to buy it," said the oldest girl, fourteen-year-old Lydia.

The others said their folks couldn't afford it either. And wasn't it terrible not to have sugar to sweeten cakes and cookies with?

"We can't even get honey any more," said thirteen-year-old Mary.

"We can't either!" cried others.

"But aren't there any bee trees here?" asked Molly. "I should think there would be."

"Father said there were," Lydia replied. "But if a man found one, he kept the honey for his own family."

"How did you get honey for your cookies, Mrs. Irvine?" twelve-year-old Susan asked politely. "Mother will want to know," she added.

"So will my mother!" cried twelve-year-old Betsy.

"The sweetening was a present from Molly's family," Mrs. Irvine replied. Then she went upstairs so she wouldn't be asked more questions.

"May I take a cake to Cynthia?" Sarah asked. "I live across the street from her."

"Of course. Take several," answered Molly.

Now the party was over, and the girls had gone home. Molly was happy—she knew she had made friends. They had all asked her to come to see them. She wished she could tell her mother and father about it. It would make them a little happier at least.

146

Mrs. Irvine and Molly talked about the party while they cleared up the kitchen.

"We can't bake any more sugar cakes for parties," Mrs. Irvine said. "The girls asked too many questions."

Molly laughed. "Oh!" she exclaimed soon after. "Here is the package of cakes Sarah was going to take to Cynthia! She forgot them."

"It is strange Cynthia didn't come."

"Maybe she didn't feel well."

"Maybe. But the Flemings should have sent some word."

A few minutes later Sarah returned. She had come back for the cookies. No, she couldn't come in. Her mother had said she couldn't.

"Here they are." Molly handed the package to her with a smile.

Sarah took it and turned to go. Then she stopped. "I've got something to tell you," she said. "It's about Cynthia. I know why she didn't come. Mother just told me what Cynthia's mother said."

"Was Cynthia ill?"

"No, indeed! She was just as well as I am. That wasn't the reason at all."

"What was it then?"

"Oh, she said you were a hired girl."

"A what?" Molly had never heard those words before.

"A hired girl. Don't you understand? You have to work for your living. Mrs. Fleming said Cynthia couldn't be friends with you."

"Then she can't eat my cakes!" cried Molly angrily. "Give them to me."

"But I told Cynthia I'd get them."

"She can't have them!" Molly took the package from Sarah and went back into the kitchen. Sarah left in a hurry.

"I heard what she said, Molly. I was proud

of you," said Mrs. Irvine. "I was glad you had so much spunk."

"It's the Dutch in me, Mother says."

"It's splendid. It shows you won't let anyone run over you. But don't pay any attention to Sarah. She was never very smart."

"Maybe not, but she told the truth. I know that. Cynthia's mother did say it. Do you think the other girls will be allowed to be friendly with me?"

"Of course. Their mothers won't pay any attention to Mrs. Fleming. She's different from the rest of us. She has a big house, servants, fine furniture, and fine clothes."

"I don't suppose she would let Cynthia wear a work dress, would she?"

"Oh my, no! That would really be terrible. The mountains would fall down!"

"What about wooden shoes?"

"Never! The world would come to an end!"

Finally she had Molly smiling, and she thought the matter was ended. In fact she told the doctor it was. But that night they heard Molly sobbing.

"She is afraid the other girls will snub her, William."

"Do you think they will?"

"Well, Mrs. Fleming might influence their mothers."

"It's a shame! Molly is a fine girl."

"It was a very cruel thing for Mrs. Fleming to say."

"It was a cruel thing to do, too—to keep Cynthia from coming to the party."

"I won't let anyone snub Molly. I'd rather take her home. Don't you think we should?"

"I do, Anne. I certainly do. But it will be some time before I can go. I can't leave my patients just now."

"We could send her back with some of our friends, couldn't we?"

"I'm sure we could. Someone will be going east before long."

"Listen! She's still sobbing. The poor child—and so far away from home. I'm really to blame, William. I persuaded her to come here." Then Anne Irvine began to sob.

"You are not to blame, my dear," the good doctor told his wife. "We all thought Molly would be happy here. Don't worry now. We'll find a way to get her home."

Taxes and
Masked Men

THEN something happened the next day that changed the plans to send Molly home. It was the news that Dr. Irvine brought at noon.

"Well," he said gravely, "the secret about Richard Fleming has been told at last. We wondered what he did for a living. Now we know. He began to collect taxes yesterday. He's one of the King's Tory tax collectors!"

"So that's how the Flemings have lived so fine! That's why he didn't buy land here!"

"That's the reason. The governor has given him the right to collect our taxes for the Indian War. And every citizen in Carlisle is angry.

They say it is more than we ought to pay. They say he knows we can't pay it. But he is demanding it anyway."

"What will they do?—What will you do?"

"I know what we should do. We should refuse to pay, as they did in New Jersey."

"Did Father refuse?" asked Molly.

"He might have. A traveler has just brought the news. Some farmers near Trenton threatened to tar and feather a tax collector. He left in a hurry—didn't even remember his money bag."

"Hooray!" cried Molly.

"The traveler said this was going on all over New Jersey and in many parts of Pennsylvania. Shopkeepers and teamsters were as angry as farmers. And tax collectors were running away like rabbits."

"Wouldn't Joshua like to hear that!"

"He'll hear, Molly. And he should be proud

to know that other men are going to fight the King's unjust taxes, just as he is doing."

"I hope you men here will do some fighting yourselves," said Mrs. Irvine.

"We will. Richard Fleming will be visited tonight by masked men. He can leave town or take the consequences."

"Tar and feathers?" asked Molly.

"I'm not saying."

"Will you be with them?" asked Mrs. Irvine.

"That you will never know. No one must know who the men are. Their names might be told. And the King's officers might hear them. So you see it's better for you not to know."

"We might be questioned," said Mrs. Irvine.

"And if we don't know anything, we can't tell it," said Molly.

"There's one thing you'll both have to know," said the doctor. "The men are counting on you to make the masks. Thirty will be needed."

"Of course we'll make them, won't we, Molly?"

"Of course!"

"I have some old sheets that will do. You'll want holes for nose and eyes."

"Yes, and strings to tie them on. Can you have them ready by evening?"

"Yes indeed!"

Just at dusk that evening thirty masked men met at the stone quarry and marched to the Fleming house. Some carried flaming torches. Others carried muskets.

One man had a bucket of tar. Another had a large bag of feathers. They stood by their leader as he rapped on the door. They were the ones Mr. Fleming saw when he opened it.

He knew what it meant, and his face turned pale. Mrs. Fleming, who was just behind him, screamed.

"We've come to pay our war taxes," said the leader sharply. "You'll find them in this bucket and bag. We'll give you a sample—if you'd like to be paid that way."

"No—no—I'll leave. But I must have a little time. I must make plans for my family."

"Your family will go with you. We don't want Tories here."

"We'll leave in the morning."

"You'll leave now. We'll give you twenty minutes."

"But, sir, we can't pack our clothes in so short a time. We need more."

156

"Twenty minutes and no longer."

"But it will take that long to hitch the horses to the coach."

"We'll hitch them ourselves."

In twenty minutes the Flemings' coach was leaving, and the Fleming family was in it. Their fine furniture and clothes had to be left behind.

MOLLY BECOMES A HEROINE

The story about Sarah and Molly and the cookies was being told all over town. And everyone was laughing at it. But they were also praising Molly.

"Good for her!" exclaimed a stonecutter. "She wasn't feeding any Tories."

"She fired her guns right away," said a gunmaker. "She gave them a good blast, too."

"She's a girl after my own heart," said an old soldier. "She's a fighter. She'll be up and shooting before the enemy even has a chance to draw his gun."

"She's a fine girl," said a neighbor. "She's as honest as the day is long. She's smart about work, too. She seems to know how to do everything."

So Molly became a heroine. People said they were proud to have her in Carlisle. The girls all wanted to give parties for her, even tattletale Sarah. She didn't know what a heroine was. Nevertheless, she would give a party anyway.

Lydia gave the first party. The girls were there, working on their samplers. But they weren't talking about their needlework. They were still excited about the Flemings.

"Where did they go, Lydia?" asked Betsy.

"Father said they would join other Tories some place. No patriot would take them in."

"Oh, well, we won't have to pay any more taxes now," said Sarah.

"But we will," declared Rachel. "That was just the war tax the men refused to pay. They are willing to pay other taxes when times grow better."

"Would they pay the tax on sugar?" Molly asked.

The girls didn't know. But they agreed the King ought to spend American tax money in America.

"If he did we'd have better roads," said Lydia. "Then the things we need wouldn't cost so much. Pewter dishes, for instance, and salt."

Sarah giggled. "What has a road to do with dishes and salt?"

"It takes a long time to haul a load out here. It takes twice as long as it would on good roads."

"Of course!" cried the others.

"And the teamsters have to be paid for their time and the expense of the trip."

"Certainly!" the girls agreed.

Sarah was still puzzled. So the girls tried again to explain.

They said the journey wouldn't cost half so much if it could be made in half the time. The teamster wouldn't eat half so much and neither would his horses.

"But what has that to do with dishes and salt?" asked Sarah.

The girls gave up, and Lydia changed the subject. "I'm going to do what you did, Molly. I'm going to find work and help my father pay his taxes."

"So am I!" cried others.

"I don't know what I could do," said Sarah. "My father is a blacksmith."

"Why don't you learn to shoe horses?" asked Molly.

Sarah shook her head. "I asked him if I could do that. He said I'd swallow his nails."

The girls laughed. Then Lydia and her mother

brought the refreshments. There was delicious hot Scotch bread with butter. And there were mugs of fresh buttermilk.

The girls showed they liked both. They didn't leave a crumb on their plates nor one drop of milk in their mugs.

"I don't know what to have at my party," said Sarah. "I can't have cakes like Molly. And my mother is Irish."

"What do you mean?" asked Lydia

"I mean, she can't make Scotch bread."

"Don't have anything," said Molly. "We don't have to eat."

"Don't tell her that," said Betsy. "She won't have anything."

That evening Molly asked Mrs. Irvine if there would really be a school this fall.

"Yes, and there will be a good teacher. I've just had a letter. My cousin, Ralph Remy, is coming to teach."

"Oh! I'm glad! I want to learn to write. I want to tell Mother about these parties and the girls. She'll laugh when she hears about Sarah."

"Could your mother read a letter written in English?"

"She'll get someone to read it to her. And I know just what she'll say. 'John, this girl Sarah can't understand about taxes. What do you think of that?' "

"What will your father say?"

" 'Let the girl find out the way our girl did. Let her outgrow her clothes and not be able to buy any more. She'll learn all about taxes then.' "

Molly Goes to the Fort

DR. AND MRS. Irvine were eating supper when Molly came back from Sarah's party. She said she was sorry she was so late, but they had to wait for the refreshments.

"What did she have?" Mrs. Irvine asked.

"Nothing."

"But you said you had to wait."

"We did, until she told us she didn't have anything to eat. She had forgotten to tell her mother we were coming. And her mother went visiting."

"Couldn't Sarah have cooked something alone?"

"She said her mother wouldn't let her. She

163

always forgot the salt or burned the food or did something she shouldn't."

"I'm glad you are not like that, Molly."

"So am I," the doctor agreed. "You know how to make things taste good, Molly. And by the way, Anne, I'd like to have some of her good hoecakes for breakfast."

While the doctor was getting ready the next morning, Molly was frying the cakes. Mrs. Irvine was coming in from the springhouse with milk and butter.

"Mrs. Irvine," said Molly softly, "I've made the sugar sirup."

"Don't put it on the table yet. Wait till I draw in the latchstring. We don't want anyone walking in on us while we eat."

Now breakfast was over, but the doctor wasn't through praising it. "The food was fit for a king," he said. "But I don't mean King George, my dear ladies."

164

"I should hope not," said Mrs. Irvine with a smile. "Not King George."

"I'd burn his cakes," declared Molly.

There was a knock at the kitchen door. Molly quickly took the sirup from the table and hid it under a kettle. Then Mrs. Irvine went to the door and opened it.

A soldier was on the steps—a sergeant from Fort Lowther. He said the commander wanted Dr. Irvine at the fort as soon as possible. Soldiers had arrived last night. Many of them had fever this morning.

The doctor went to his office for his medicines. The sergeant explained further to Mrs. Irvine. "These men were Indian fighters. They've been in the garrison at Fort Pitt ever since the Indian War ended. They're going back home."

"Was one of them Joseph Ludwig?" asked Molly. "He is my brother."

"I don't know their names. The doctor can find out. I'll speak to him about it."

The doctor was ready now, and they left at once. The sergeant forgot about Joseph Ludwig. So when Dr. Irvine came back he couldn't tell Molly anything.

"He wasn't among the soldiers I treated. But I haven't seen them all. You can go back with me this afternoon. I'll ask the commander about him. He will know."

An hour later they were in that officer's room. He was looking at a long list of names. "Yes, here is his name—Lieutenant Joseph Ludwig. I'll take you to him, Miss. The doctor is too busy."

On the way, Molly asked if Joseph would be able to talk with her.

"Oh, yes, he can talk. But he's weak. He's been ill with fever."

He led her into a room with bunks around the walls. In every bunk was a soldier. Molly noticed how young they were. She noticed also that not a single one was smiling.

The commander stopped at a bunk in a corner. The soldier there had his face to the wall.

"Well, Lieutenant," said the officer, "here's company to see you."

A blond and handsome young man turned his head. He seemed dazed for a moment. Then he smiled and stretched out his hand. "Molly!" he said softly. "Molly!"

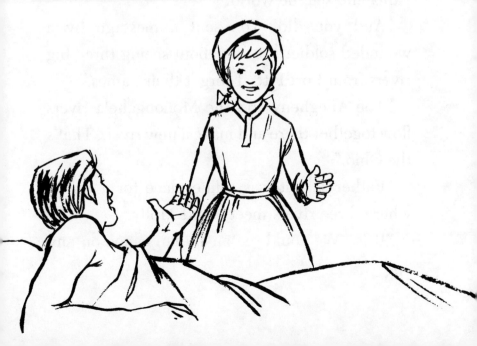

The girl bent over him and kissed his cheek. Then she sat on a stool and talked quietly. She explained how she happened to be there, but she tried to make it funny. She didn't mention hard times or taxes. She said their mother and father thought it would be wonderful for her to travel with Dr. and Mrs. Irvine. "They said I might never have another chance," she added.

"That's what I thought when I joined the army. I wanted to go out to western Pennsylvania and see the world."

"And you did! You sent a message by a wounded soldier. It was about seeing three big rivers from Fort Pitt. I forgot their names."

"The Allegheny and the Monongahela rivers flow together there and make a new river. That's the Ohio."

"Father said it was a fine place for a fort— where three rivers meet," said Molly.

"It is. We could see an Indian canoe on any

one of them. That's the reason Fort Pitt was built there."

"I'd give anything to see those rivers."

"I'd trade all three of them for the creek back of our barn."

"Amen!" cried a soldier in the next bunk.

"Why, Joseph, didn't you like it out there?"

"Ask me if I liked to be hit by Indian arrows."

"I meant, didn't you like the scenery?"

"Trees don't look so grand when you know there's an enemy behind them."

"That's the truth," said a voice from a bunk.

Joseph went on, "If I ever get home I'll never leave again. I've seen enough."

"But you didn't like cows," Molly said.

"I love them now."

"You didn't like to milk. You didn't like them switching their tails in your face."

"They can switch their tails all over me from now on," Joseph declared.

"Me, too!" exclaimed a soldier.

"Me, too!" cried others.

Molly knew they were in dead earnest, so she didn't even smile. She just went on talking. "I know how you can stop that switching. All you have to do is to get rid of flies."

"It can't be done, sister."

"I did it. I put a large cloth over the cow's back. Then I spread honey on it. And the honey caught the flies."

"I wish I had thought of that."

Then it was time for Molly to leave.

"Come again tomorrow, Molly," said Joseph.

"I will. I'll come every day you are here," Molly promised.

THE SOLDIERS LIKED MOLLY'S STORIES

The next noon Dr. Irvine said Joseph was better. His voice was stronger and he was happier. "Your visit lifted his spirits, Molly, and the spirits of many of the other soldiers. Medicines alone don't always cure people who are ill. Joseph needed more than medicine."

She knew he was better that afternoon, but he was still too weak to talk much. Molly wondered what she could tell him. Then she thought of Melissa, and she asked Joseph if he remembered her.

"Of course. She was my pet cat."

"I wish you could have seen what she did one morning. I saw her stretched out under the gooseberry bush in the garden. Her kitten was stretched out beside her."

"Were they asleep?"

"No indeed! Their eyes were as big as saucers. I knew Melissa was up to something so I sat down and watched. Pretty soon I saw a bird flying over the bush. She would fly away, and then she would come back. I could tell she had a

171

nest there and that she wanted to go to it. But she flew too high for the cats. So they waited."

"All ready to spring, of course!"

"Of course. At last the bird flew lower, and the cats sprang at once. But they missed. The bird flew away. And what do you think Melissa did then?"

"I don't know. What?"

"She was so mad she boxed the kitten's ear."

Joseph didn't smile this time. He laughed. And the other soldiers laughed with him.

"Mellisa didn't want to blame herself. So she blamed the kitten. She's exactly like some people. They always blame the other fellow," said Joseph.

"That's a fact," declared a near-by soldier. "Melissa is the army all over. If a private can't get exactly what he wants to eat, he blames the corporal."

Other soldiers went on:

172

"And the corporal blames the sergeant."

"And the sergeant blames the lieutenant."

"And the lieutenant blames the captain."

"And the captain blames the major."

"And the major blames the general."

There was silence. It was the youngest soldier's turn, but he didn't speak.

"Go on! Go on!" they shouted.

"It's the general's turn," a boy reminded him.

"I know, but he's at the top. He can't blame anyone but himself, and he wouldn't do that, would he?"

"No!" shouted every man together.

"Well then, who would he blame?"

"The Indians," Molly replied.

Then they all laughed. And when Molly left they asked her to tell another story tomorrow.

She asked Dr. Irvine about it that night. "Would it be all right to tell them about my calf and the fair?"

"Yes, indeed! These boys are all homesick. They've been out there in the wilderness too long. Your stories will help to cure them. Tell them about your calf. Then tell them about the barge and the balloon."

The soldiers liked both stories. They were glad Blossom won the prize. They wanted to know who had the sense to slit the balloon.

"I just happened to think of it," said Molly.

"You think quickly, Miss Molly," said one. And the others agreed.

Another time she told the soldiers about the night at the Red Fox Inn.

"We might have to stop there," Joseph said. "We'll have to sleep on our muskets, boys."

"If you don't, they'll steal your canteens," declared Molly.

Her story about the tax collector excited them. They said Americans shouldn't have to pay all the expenses of the Indian War. England ought to pay most of them herself. The King had been grabbing land from the Indians. It was his fault the Indians fought the white men.

There was one story Molly did not tell. She hadn't even told Joseph, and he was leaving tomorrow with the others. This story was about the smugglers and the patriot who was their leader. This secret she would keep forever.

Molly's Courage in Battle

TWELVE years had passed. It was now 1778, and again soldiers were passing the Ludwig dairy farm. This time they were not going west to fight Indians.

These troops were marching east to fight English soldiers. They were part of General George Washington's army of patriots. They had been fighting with him since 1776.

This was the year when American patriots rose up against King George. Let him send his army to America. The patriots would raise an army of their own.

John Ludwig's three sons were among the first

to join. They were with the regiment passing the farm now. They were all proud to be fighting in the defense of their country.

They wanted to stop, but there was no time. Their troops were pursuing an English army. It would be a race to catch up with it before it reached New York. The English were far ahead of the Americans. The patriots must march fast.

General Washington had made his plans for a battle. He was determined to make the English turn and fight.

The three Ludwig officers saw their mother and father at the gate. They saw their sister Molly at the roadside with a bucket of water and a dipper. They smiled and waved, and each called out as he passed.

"We'll catch them!" shouted Lieutenant Joshua.

"We'll fight them!" shouted Captain Joseph.

"We'll lick them, too!" shouted Sergeant Carl.

After these troops passed, Molly watched for the Pennsylvania regiment. Her husband, John Hays, was a gunner in the artillery.

The colonel was Dr. William Irvine. He was coming now on his black horse. She hoped he would stop. She wanted to ask him about John.

Yes, he had seen her! He was crossing the road. A moment later Colonel Irvine reined up his horse and was leaning down to talk. "Your husband was able to come today, Molly. He's with the artillery under General Nathanael Greene."

"But is he strong enough to fire a cannon, Colonel? He has hardly had time to recover from a fever."

"He declared he was fit. He was determined to come."

"Can't I follow his company? I want to take care of him if he is hurt."

"A battlefield is no place for a woman. Stay

here or go to Anne in Princeton. She wants you." Then he rode away to join his troops.

Now came the artillery. Molly saw her husband on a cannon carriage. He waved to her, but there was no chance for him to stop. She was so disappointed that tears came to her eyes.

"They'll have to slow down at the hill," said her father. "John might come back."

John came running back. "I'll have a minute with you, Molly. I'll join them at the bottom of the hill."

"John, I'm afraid you'll be hurt in this battle."

"We have doctors."

"There weren't half enough in the other battles you were in. I want to take care of you if you're wounded."

"No, Molly. Stay here with your parents. I'll come when the battle is over. I can get a leave from Colonel Irvine. Now good-by! I must be on my way."

180

He ran toward the hill, and Molly joined her parents.

"This is the hottest June day I ever saw," declared her father. "If it's this hot tomorrow, it will be terrible for the soldiers."

"I'm afraid it will be," said Gretchen. "Look how the leaves curl up. That's a sure sign of hot weather."

"My brothers can stand it," said Molly. "They are used to the sun. But John always did inside work till he went into the army. He won't be able to fire his cannon long."

"That's hot work even in cool weather," said Mr. Ludwig.

"I know that is true, Father. I watched John and the other gunners last winter. I lived near his camp at Valley Forge, you remember. I went there every few days."

"You came all the way from Carlisle to be with him," said her mother.

"Yes, and I'll be with him again," declared Molly. "If he falls, I'll be there to help him. I could give him water. I could keep him alive."

"There will be many soldiers wanting water on the battlefield."

"I'll try to give it to them."

"You'll be risking your life, Molly."

"My husband and my brothers are risking their lives, Mother."

"That's true," said John Ludwig. "You may take my horse, Molly."

An hour later Molly Hays was on the way. Tied to her saddle was a large pewter pitcher. It was the same one she had used so many years ago to fill the soldiers' canteens.

MOLLY IN THE BATTLE OF MONMOUTH

The English army had not been able to reach New York. The American troops had caught up with them in the next county. On the evening of June 27, 1778, both armies had camped near the town of Freehold in Monmouth County, New Jersey.

On June 28, the battle began at noon. General Washington ordered his gunners on a hill to drive the English from the open fields below. Their cannon fire must not stop till the enemy retreated.

The infantry had the same orders. And every soldier fought to win. Then came another enemy. Silently but steadily this enemy came. It was a force the patriots couldn't fight. No shots were fired, but men dropped all over the battlefield.

This enemy was the heat. It had been hot at daybreak. It grew hotter and hotter. By noon it was almost 100 degrees. And there was also the heat of the battle, of powder and shot and shells.

Hundreds of soldiers could not stand it. They fell on the ground by the dead. They knew they would also cease to live if help did not come soon. But who was there to help?

Stretcher-bearers would not come till the battle was over. That might not be until night. The men could not last that long. They gave up all hope.

Then some heard a woman's voice close beside them. Were they dreaming? No woman could be on this battleground. It was fever, they thought, the fever from thirst.

"Let me give you a drink," said a voice. "I'll hold up your head. Come, now, drink from my pitcher."

They drank and lived. Then other fallen soldiers drank from that pitcher. And others and others until it was empty.

"I will get more," the woman said. "The well is near. It is just across the road. Call me if you want another drink. Just say 'Molly'—I will come to you."

The sick men whispered her name to others. Before long many feeble voices were calling, "Molly! Molly! Pitcher! Pitcher!" Sometimes these calls were just "Molly Pitcher, Molly Pitcher."

These men were too weak to separate the words. Others who heard them thought this was the woman's name. So they called for Molly Pitcher, too. And Molly Hays didn't stop them. She didn't care what they called her.

Her only thought was to keep them alive. She went out where cannon balls were falling. She went out into the smoke and blazing sun. She did not think of her own safety.

A hundred fallen men were kept alive by that water. Some were able to fight again. All blessed the woman who had saved them.

As Molly went back and forth to the well, she passed near her husband's cannon. On every trip she looked to see if he was still firing. Suddenly she missed him. At once she ran to his cannon. He was lying beside it. But he was not wounded. He had been overcome by the heat.

She gave him water. She bathed his face, but she couldn't revive him. He was unable to stand.

Now an orderly came running. "Why is this gun silent?" he asked. "Where is the gunner?"

Molly Hays pointed to her husband on the ground. "He can't fire another shot," she said. "He is exhausted."

"Is there no other gunner here? This cannon must be fired! That is the General's order."

"There is no other gunner. All have been killed or wounded. My husband was the last one able to fire."

"What can I do? General Washington said the cannon fire must not cease."

"I'll fire it!" cried Molly. "I've watched my husband. I know I can swab and load."

She seized the rammer. She swabbed and loaded and fired. The orderly watched her.

"Well done!" he cried. "No gunner could do better! I'll report to General Washington!"

The bullets fell around Molly. But she swabbed and loaded and fired. The hot sun blazed down on her, but she swabbed and loaded and fired.

Her dress was black from gunpowder. There were smudges on her face and hands. She paid no attention. Her cannon must be fired!

The battle raged on till dark. Then both armies ceased firing. Stretcher-bearers came for the wounded. John Hays was carried to the field hospital.

Molly couldn't follow him because she had to

stay by her cannon. A new battle would begin at sunrise, and every gunner must be ready.

However, with daylight came a surprise. The English army had fled during the night. They had had enough.

As soon as Molly heard this she started to the hospital. But an orderly stopped her. "General Washington wishes you to come to his headquarters, Mrs. Hays."

"But my dress, my face, my hands——"

"The General will understand. He knows that you have been engaged in battle."

Presently Molly was facing the commander-in-chief and his generals. General Washington took her powder-stained hand in his. He smiled at her and spoke kindly.

"Mrs. Hays, the courage you showed yesterday has never been equalled by any woman. Your kindness has never been surpassed. You were an angel of mercy to suffering men. You were a pillar of strength at the cannon, with the skill of an experienced gunner.

"We dealt the English a heavy blow. Without your help we might not have succeeded. Therefore, I make you a sergeant in this army. And I now pin this badge of honor upon you."

There was silence until this was over. Then a thousand soldiers began to cheer.

"Hooray for Sergeant Molly!" they cried. "Hooray for Molly Pitcher!"

The other generals shook hands with her. They called her a brave woman and a kind one.

"All America will be proud of you," declared General Knox. "Not only today and tomorrow, but forever."

"You are a heroine, Sergeant Molly," said General Nathanael Greene. "Your name will go down in history."

General Lafayette was so delighted that he asked to honor Molly by having her review his troops. He formed the men into two lines. As Molly left, she walked between the two lines of French soldiers. Every one of them saluted her as she passed.

And again she heard a thousand voices cry, "Hooray for Sergeant Molly! Hooray for Molly Pitcher!"